I0145734

REACHING THE PROMISED LAND

UNWRAP YOUR SPIRITUAL PRESENT

Compiled by

Nachum Shaw

Promised Land

JERUSALEM   LONDON   NEW YORK

For further information:

Promised Land Publishers

Apt. 8, 5 Gimmel Alroyi St.

Jerusalem 9210808

ISRAEL

or

Promised Land Publishers

8 Woodville Road

London NW11 9TN

ENGLAND

or

Promised Land Publishers

67 Wood Hollow Lane

New Rochelle

NY 10804

USA

Email: promisedland920@gmail.com

www.promisedlandpublishers.com

CONTENTS

Foreword

This book is an inspiring compilation that presents various aspects of the unfolding and elevating process which is leading us to the fulfillment of the magnificent promise offered to all humanity, and given to us by God in the Torah, of everyone living together at peace on this earth. This solid assurance is echoed and underscored by the astounding divinely-given visions received by the Hebrew prophets, that we can all read, of the wonderful future that they foresee for the whole world; the harmonious state of existence that will prevail in the wake of the global raising of God-consciousness that is bound to follow the longed-for rebuilding of Jerusalem, and the ultimate return of the Children of Israel to the Promised Land.

Included are chapters that focus on how to reach our own personal promised land of self-realization, by doing good deeds, helping the less fortunate and needy, divesting ourselves of acquired negative character traits and refining our positive ones. *Reaching the Promised Land* also explains how through introspection and meditation we can manage to uncover more and more of our inner spiritual treasure, that is within us all, here and now, thus getting to experience ever-greater levels of the joy of living in the knowledge that we are divine souls, truly made in the image of our Creator.

Through us, the people who received the Torah at Sinai, continuing to remain faithful to God, and thereby fulfilling our role as a light to the nations, this book envisions every country in turn also becoming a promised land, as it discovers its own place in the beautiful mosaic of a transformed world, with caring people everywhere, conscious of the Divine, living happily in a kind and loving way.

A father once explained sadly to the holy Baal Shem Tov that his son had abandoned God "What shall I do, Rabbi?" he asked in despair. And the Baal Shem Tov answered, "Love him even more than ever!"

INTRODUCTION

The Book of Genesis begins with the vivid account of God creating the heaven and the earth; following comes the revelation that we are living souls made in God's image. We then discover the promised blessings for all of humanity that are destined to unfold. Everyone's invited to see this exquisite vision through the lens of God's chosen people, Israel, whose role is to be the prototype of what all mankind will ultimately become.

God gave us the Torah via Moses on Mount Sinai. The Torah (meaning teaching or instruction) is God's user's manual for how to live a good, correct and an illuminated life in this world. It is the spiritual guide and outline for humanity of how to trace our way back to the early perfection of Eden, the idyllic destination that God has sworn we will arrive at. So it is truly eye-opening to discover that these holy writings that inform us of a journey to the Promised Land and the wonderful future that awaits mankind, remarkably, make an allusion to this in the very first sentence.

Looking for some hint of where the Promised Land is encoded within these first few words, we would be delighted if we could discover that both the words 'promise' and 'land' are actually alluded to there. Well, guess what? They certainly are!

In the Holy Tongue, as we can see, the roots of the words 'promise' (sh'va) and 'seven' (sh'va) are identical. As is extremely well known, the Bible starts with the words, "In the beginning God created the heaven and the earth." In the original, this is rendered as, 'Bereishit bara Elokim et hashamayim v'et ha'aretz' (Genesis 1:1). As just mentioned, in the Torah seven and promise are spelled the same. Seven = sheva = **promise**. Now, we find that the 7th word is 'ha'aretz (the earth or **land**). The Promised Land is beautifully intimated, right at the very beginning!

Signaling the Divine plan, 'ha'aretz' can refer to both the land of Israel (Eretz Yisrael) and also the whole world. This control experiment that God set up, to refine a 'kingdom of priests and a holy nation' to Him, is for the sole purpose of raising up in this world a people (Israel), who from the very outset were intended to be the forerunners of what all of humanity are to become; self-aware beings enjoying rich and wonderful lives, caring for one another, each one reaching their own promised land.

The dawning of this promised era for us all, that will herald a time of serenity, joy and enlightenment, could indeed occur at any moment, and so we are assured, certainly by the seventh millennium - and we are now very near the end of the sixth. This promised time is right on the horizon.

This is all drawn from an allegorical understanding of the first chapter of Genesis, where 'Adam' can not only mean 'man' but can also allude to being 'mankind', and the first six days could also be read as 6000 years - 'For a thousand years in Your eyes are as a yesterday...' (Psalms 90:4). When mankind has ultimately developed enough and reached full maturity - toward the end of this sixth 'day' we then become ready to enter the promised seventh 'day' (millennium) of peace, harmony and ever greater degrees of experiencing the wonders of our God-given existence. A truly profound reading of the Torah reveals that this state of blissful knowledge is accessible to each individual right now, if we only look deeply within, meditating lovingly on our own divine souls, and the souls of everyone else - "the world is built with kindness" (Psalms 89:3).

Just as the viewing of time as being the 'fourth dimension' catapulted scientists with a great quantum leap into a whole new conception of reality, so too are we shortly about to experience a new transcendental change - in our perception of reality. We are quickly approaching this critical point in history where, even now, we find ourselves teetering on the verge of a totally transformed level of existence - about to levitate into what could be called the 'fifth dimension'. In this dimension, our experience of space and time will be totally transformed as we behold a world full of kindness and truth uncovered. Seeing this 'fifth dimension' (the dimension of the soul) is the promised vision of the world that awaits us, that was long ago foretold to us by the Hebrew prophets – a world where all the nations together will finally recognize the Creator of us all, and thankfully discover the purpose for which we were originally created – to make of this world a heaven right here on earth.

Do You Mind?

For humanity to mature, to move forward and find itself in a world where everyone's perception of reality will be a truly joyful one, it is evident that our priority must be to first attend to the needs of those who are currently dealing with various ongoing problems, whose lives are difficult and who are disturbed.

In our world, there are many people who are beset by confusion, anxiety, depression or a personality disorder. Many of these people who look for assistance, often find themselves seeking relief and solutions from members of the psychiatric profession, or people calling themselves psychotherapists.

While these professionals and therapists are genuinely motivated by good will and the desire to help and heal their patients or clients, their treatments are most commonly derived from their study of the modern-day "science" called psychology – a hit or miss patchwork of theories, some more effective than others.

They seek to help the sufferer discover the causes of their condition, and then try to address the symptoms of the dis-ease, through a variety of means. Sometimes prescribing medication, they may offer counseling and also employ various therapies, but tragically, in general, they fail to properly grasp what the true nature of men, women and children is – that we are actually living souls created by God (Genesis 2:7).

Instead of just loving these living souls, and listening to their concerns with infinite patience, there is a tendency in the profession to merely see these "cases" just as beings endowed with numerous primitive needs and wants that are derived from some underlying archetypal genetic programming, along with characters and thought processes formed over time by historical traumas.

Addressing these imagined imprints and maladies, psychology has developed techniques that attempt to "correct" dysfunctional people by reprogramming them so that they can live a bearable existence and become useful members of society.

Within this mechanistic worldview, human beings are conceived of as bodies, each one having a mind of its own. Yet, nobody has been able to locate this "mind"; the intellectuals claim that it is in the brain, the romantics insist it is in the heart. Psychology studies this "mind" and the thoughts that it generates, and psychiatrists and psychotherapists attempt to treat this "mind", even though nobody has ever proved that their idea of a "mind" actually exists. This faith in its existence is something akin to a religious belief system.

This quasi-science named psychology, and its offshoots, psychiatry, psychoanalysis and psychotherapy, are all etymologically derived from the Greek word *psyche*; and this prefix, their practitioners tell us, means something associated with the myth that they call the "mind".

Despite its modern connotation, the literal meaning of *psyche* is not to be translated as being a separate, disembodied mind (a concept that would completely baffle the ancient Greeks). The actual translation of the word *psyche* is in fact SOUL.

From this, we see that all these professionals who despite their noble, yet floundering attempts to help and heal their patients and clients, had after all (probably subconsciously), chosen the correct prefix to name each of their "sciences", even if they offered them far from optimal treatments. They had unwittingly, actually identified the source of someone's bewilderment, anxiety, confusion or depression, as not being that of a fictitious "mind", rather the suffering of a divine soul - made in God's image (Genesis 1:26).

So the tragic consequences of this misapprehension of a person's true identity, as a living soul, are that countless people have been wrongly diagnosed as having disorders of the mind, and are then ascribed the term "mentally ill", when in actual fact their suffering is due to them being very troubled souls, needing patient love and great understanding.

Subsequently, numerous courses of "treatment" (medication and/or therapies) are employed with these suffering souls, that very rarely address what the true cause of their suffering is; while incidentally keeping the psychiatrists and psychotherapists well-funded with a guaranteed source of income, having patients and clients on their books for a very long time, maybe even for life.

Ultimately, rather than being dependent on others, a healthy and well-functioning individual is someone who has discovered that the key to one's salvation, tranquility and happiness is given to each one of us as a divine inheritance. Meanwhile, in the first place, troubled souls need to be showered with much care, attention and understanding for them to be able to eventually realize this truth for themselves.

We are all born with the ability to distinguish between good and evil behavior, to decide to be generous or selfish, to care or be indifferent, and to be kind or be cruel. True moral and spiritual education is learning how to choose the better alternative every time.

It is in this very commonality of human potential, to do good or bad, as acts consciously decided by our free will, that the remedy for any disorder or suffering in the lives of every person is to be found.

Acknowledging our own responsibility for how we respond to all of our life situations is the first step in recovering from maladies of the soul. Yet, what is most often lacking in the established "mental health" worldview, is the recognition that we are all pure souls, endowed by our Creator with infinite resources, able to rise to meet every challenge that life throws at us, and deal with and overcome them all.

When people are near the point of despair, the last thing they need is to be made to believe that they are not like everyone else, and that they are suffering from some form of "mental illness". What they require is to receive the loving assurance that they are neither obligated to anybody, nor helpless victims, and that not so deep down they actually have the God-given ability to liberate themselves from their self-imposed prisons.

Even when the existence of the soul is acknowledged, it is the lack of recognition in the world of psychology that the soul is created by God, and has unlimited potential, that results in such a poor rate of success in psychiatrists' and therapists' efforts to help their patients or clients. Never can the old expression, "the road to hell is paved with good intentions" have been more appropriately used than when applied to all the misdiagnoses that these well-meaning people arrive at, when trying to be of assistance to these sad individuals.

One such person was Freud, a product of an assimilated and Reform Jewish background, an avowed atheist, who nevertheless, paradoxically and perplexingly insisted on the existence of the soul as being central to his method and teachings. Yet, there is a virtual absence of any consideration of the presence of the soul in the later treatment by practitioners of psychoanalysis, even though it was clearly stated that it was specifically the soul that its founder was encouraging others to discover. Maybe an atheist propounding the existence of a soul was not exactly convincing.

Added to this, the misrepresentation of what Freud originally intended to convey in his writings by later psychoanalysts hardly mentioning the soul, came about through the secular and materialistic worldview that prevailed and still prevails among the medical fraternity, and inaccurate translations of Freud's works. As one of his hero-worshippers, Bruno Bettelheim relates in his book *Freud and Man's Soul*:

"In *The Interpretation of Dreams* (1900), which opened to our understanding not just the meaning of dreams but also the nature and power of the unconscious, Freud told about his arduous struggle to achieve ever greater self-awareness. In other books, he told why he felt it necessary for the rest of us to do the same. In a way, all his writings are gentle, persuasive, often brilliantly worded intimations that we, his readers, would benefit from a similar spiritual journey of self-discovery. Freud showed us how the soul could become aware of itself. To become acquainted with the lowest depth of the soul--to explore whatever personal hell we may suffer from--is not an easy undertaking. Freud's findings and, even more, the way he presents them to us give us the confidence that this demanding and potentially dangerous voyage of self-discovery will result in our becoming more fully human, so that we may no longer be enslaved without knowing it to the dark forces that reside in us. By exploring and understanding the origins and the potency of these forces, we not only become much better able to cope with them but also gain a much deeper and more compassionate understanding of our fellow man. In his work and in his writings, Freud often spoke of the soul--of its nature and structure, its development, its attributes, how it reveals itself in all we do and dream. Unfortunately, nobody who reads him in English could guess this, because nearly all his many references to the soul, and to matters pertaining to the soul, have been excised in translation.

...I became aware of this in the 1940s, when I became director of the University of Chicago's Orthogenic School, for disturbed children. The staff members I worked with were well read in Freud; they were convinced that they had made his ideas their own, and they tried to put their understanding of Freud into practice in their work with the children. The considerable theoretical understanding of unconscious processes which they had acquired from studying Freud remained exactly that: theoretical. It was of little use in helping children afflicted by severe psychiatric disorders; often it was even an impediment. It was a reasoned-out, emotionally distant understanding. What was needed was emotional closeness based on an immediate sympathetic comprehension of all aspects of the child's soul-- of what afflicted it, and why. What was needed was what Freud occasionally spoke of explicitly but much more often implicitly: a spontaneous sympathy of our unconscious with that of others, a feeling response of our soul to theirs. By reading Freud in translation, the staff members had missed all this-- one cannot be expected to gain an understanding of the soul if the soul is never mentioned.

The biggest shortcoming of the translations is that, through their use of abstractions, they make it easy for the reader to distance himself from what Freud sought to teach about the inner life of man and of the reader himself. Psychoanalysis becomes in English translation something that refers and applies to others as a system of intellectual constructs.

11

Therefore, students of psychoanalysis are not led to take it personally--they are not moved to gain access to their own unconscious and everything else within them that is most human but is nevertheless unacceptable to them.

For nearly forty years, I have taught courses in psychoanalysis to American graduate students and residents in psychiatry. Again and again, I have been made to see how seriously the English translations impede students' efforts to gain a true understanding of Freud and of psychoanalysis. Although most of the bright and dedicated students whom it has been my pleasure to teach were eager to learn what psychoanalysis is all about, they were largely unable to do so. Almost invariably, I have found that psychoanalytic concepts had become for these students a way of looking only at others, from a safe distance--nothing that had any bearing on them. They observed other people through the spectacles of abstraction, tried to comprehend them by means of intellectual concepts, never turning their gaze inward to the soul or their own unconscious. This was true even of the students who were in analysis themselves--it made no appreciable difference. Psychoanalysis had helped some of them to be more at peace with themselves and to cope with life, had helped others to free themselves of troublesome neurotic symptoms, but their misconceptions about psychoanalysis remained. Psychoanalysis as these students perceived it was a purely intellectual system--a clever, exciting game--rather than the acquisition of insights into oneself and one's own behavior which were potentially deeply upsetting. It was always someone else's unconscious they analyzed, hardly ever their own. They did not give enough thought to the fact that Freud, in order to create psychoanalysis and understand the workings of the unconscious, had had to analyze his own dreams, understand his own slips of the tongue and the reasons he forgot things or made various other mistakes.

The best explanation for these students' failure to grasp the essence of Freud's thinking is the universal wish to remain unaware of one's own unconscious. Freud, who understood very well that this would be true for his readers, tried to speak to them as directly as possible. When he wrote about himself and his patients, he wrote in a manner designed to induce the reader to recognize that he was speaking about us all--about the reader as much as about himself, his patients, and others. Freud's choice of words and his direct style serve the purpose of making the reader apply psychoanalytic insights to himself, because only from his inner experience can he fully understand what Freud was writing about.

… Of all the mistranslations of Freud's phraseology, none has hampered our understanding of his humanistic views more than the elimination of his references to the soul (die Seele).

… In the paper "The 'Uncanny' " (1919), Freud's phrase "im seelischen Unbewussten" ("in the unconscious of the soul") has been translated as "in the unconscious mind." In the same sentence, "gewisse Seiten des Seelenlebens" ("certain aspects of the life of the soul") has been rendered as "certain aspects of the mind."

Freud never faltered in his conviction that it was important to think in terms of the soul when trying to comprehend his system, because no other concept could make equally clear what he meant; nor can there be any doubt that he meant the soul, and not the mind, when he wrote "seelisch."

…There really was no reason--apart from a wish to interpret psychoanalysis as a medical specialty--for this corruption of Freud's references to the soul."

Even though Freud repeatedly spoke about delving into the soul to discover its secrets, nevertheless, through his insistent desire that his teachings be accepted as serious academic studies, a part of the humanities and also a "scientific" method, it is obvious that he himself had not recognized the real *root* of his own soul. It is evident from a study of his writings that he could never have experienced the sublime joy that flows from acknowledging the true divinity of the soul.

Tragically, despite all his genuine desire to understand human behavior, the efforts by Freud to try and distance psychoanalysis from being viewed as a sectarian practise and dubbed a "Jewish science", have themselves contributed greatly to the shrouding of the actual nature of the soul in the modern world. He never managed to shine a light on the godly soul within, due to the fact that this is something that Freud, along with most of the psychological schools, were in the dark about, and remained unaware of, because they very foolishly denied its existence. Humanism shows compassion, but, without belief in God, lacks passion.

On encountering any difficulties in life, if we can fully recognize that we are pure souls - divine in origin, and sparks of God, then we will easily manage to summon up the energy, and find the confidence and courage, to look deeply within ourselves. Afterwards, following this searching introspection to uncover any self-deception and delusions, we shall be able to once again continue to be, or for the first time become, the radiant, happy beings that we were always intended by our Creator to be.

So we see that, in order to truly be able to analyze ourselves, and thereby discover who we really are, and catch a glimpse of who we can become, we must first of all arrive at the astounding and joyful realization that we, along with every being and everything that exists, are actually created and sustained by God; all having a specific, essential and special purpose for being here.

"Taste and see that the Lord is good; fortunate is the man who trusts in Him. Fear the Lord, you His holy ones, for those who fear Him suffer no want. Young lions may want and hunger, but those who seek the Lord shall not lack any good thing. Come, children, listen to me; I will teach you the fear of the Lord. Who is the man who desires life, who loves long life wherein to see goodness? Guard your tongue from evil, and your lips from speaking deceit. Turn away from evil and do good, seek peace and pursue it."

PSALMS 34:9-14

JEWISH MYSTICISM

Excerpts from *The Jew in the Lotus* by Rodger Kamenetz

When Kabbalists read Genesis, they see not one, but four worlds being created. The four supernal worlds correspond to the four letters of God's Name – Yod, Heh, Vav, Heh.

'	Yod	Fire	Spirit	Emanation	Intellect	Atzilut
ה	Heh	Air	Mind	Creation	Knowing	Beriah
ו	Vav	Water	Heart	Formation	Feeling	Yetzirah
ה	Heh	Earth	Body	Function	Doing	Asiyah

Each of the letters represents a realm of the spirit or consciousness, namely the body, heart, mind and spirit.

In the prayer liturgy, God is described as a father, a king of kings, an almighty, but within the four worlds, cosmology, the highest contemplations avoid such imagery. The realm of nearness (Atzilut) is both full of God and empty – because at that level there is no 'thing' to be.

The name the kabbalists used for God in Atzilut is Ein Sof. This literally means no limit, or infinite. Yet in some interpretations, Ein Sof is translated as Ayin – nothing.

For instance, the thirteenth-century kabbalist Joseph Gikatilla writes, "The depth of primordial being is called Boundless. It is also called Ayin (nothing) because of its concealment from all creatures. If one asks, 'What is it?' the answer is 'Ayin', that is no one can understand anything about it."

Zalman Schachter once took a group of people to see the Lubavitcher Rebbe. One of them asked the Rebbe, "What are you good for?" And he said, "I'm not talking about myself, I'm talking about what my master was for me. He was for me a geologist of the soul. There are great treasures in the soul: there's faith, there's love, there's wisdom, all these treasures you can dig up; but if you don't know where to dig, you dig up mud – Freud – or you dig up stones – Adler. But if you want to get to the gold, which is the awe of God, and the silver, which is the love, and the diamonds, which are the faith, then you have to find the geologist of the soul, who will tell you where to dig." The Rebbe added, "But the digging you have to do yourself."

In Jewish life today, the mystical is either ignored or consigned to a distant superstitious past, and there is, at least popularly, a strongly felt dichotomy between what is considered the rational or reasonable...and the mystical.

This reflects the generally materialistic and scientific worldview in the West. As a result, we tend to read our Jewish history as though the great rabbinic sages were pure rationalists, or dry legalists. While the rabbinic sages were cautious about esoteric experiences, that very caution shows they evidently viewed Merkavah (Ezekiel's chariot) meditation as a very powerful even if possibly dangerous practise. The same Rabbi Akiva who was a great second-century Tanna, or codifier of the Talmud, was also a practitioner of Merkavah meditation. The two were intrinsic to each other because the rabbinic sages drew on a visionary experience to interpret Torah.

Likewise, Rabbi Isaac Luria of sixteenth-century Safed, is considered by Orthodox Jews to be both a Talmudic authority and a great kabbalist. So was another member of his circle, Rabbi Joseph Karo. He is known primarily today as the compiler of the *Shulchan Aruch* (the set table) – the everyday practical law for the Orthodox. But the same Joseph Karo had regular communications with a maggid, or oracular spirit, who produced automatic speech through his mouth. In other words, Joseph

Karo was, in effect, both a codifier of Jewish law and an oracular medium.

All of this history shows that the present gulf between rational and mystical, or between legalistic and magical, has not always been a factor of Jewish life. It is rather an artefact of extreme materialism.

Jonathan Omer-Man has demonstrated that the Jewish tradition ... has techniques of mental transformation..."We have a very big problem in the West. The work of transformation has been stolen from us by the psychiatrists. The work of transformation, for us is a holy path. But more and more, people who are stopped, don't go to rabbi or a priest. They go to a psychiatrist who will teach them not enlightenment, but self-satisfaction."

Jewish mysticism teaches certain techniques for raising sexual energy to celestial realms. The very first written description of Jewish meditation is found in a marriage manual, *The Holy Letter*, attributed to the kabbalist Joseph Gikatilla. As described in Rabbi Aryeh Kaplan's *Jewish Meditation*, the partners meditate throughout the sexual act, becoming aware of the spark of the Divine in the pleasure itself and elevating it to its source.

In Jewish mystical thought, then, there is a sacralisation of the erotic and an eroticization of the sacred. But this mixture of the erotic and the holy, though very salient in kabbalah, is highly suppressed in mainstream Judaism.

Judaism is definitely a householder religion. Historically, its experiments with monasticism were brief, the Essenes being the best known group. (It's not clear that all Essene groups were celibate.) Even the tzaddik or prophet, must be part of "this world". Therefore, in the Jewish context, the practise of sexual yoga (ecstatic meditation) is exclusively between husband and wife.

For many historical reasons, the door to the Jewish esoteric remains shut to most Jews. This is why an opening to the esoteric could be very important in correcting the impression that Judaism is strictly patriarchal, or that its imagery is strictly masculine. For the door closed by mainstream Judaism on the esoteric is also a door closed to the body, and to the feminine. For instance, it is interesting to read the Zoharic commentary on the verse in Genesis, "...male and female He created them." In Daniel Matt's translation, "From here we learn: Any image that does not embrace male and female is not a high and true image. ... Come and see: The Blessed Holy One does not place His abode in any place where male and female are not found together. Blessings are only found in a place where male and female are found, as it is written, He blessed them and called their name Adam on the day they were created. It is not written: He blessed him and called his name Adam. A human being is only called Adam when male and female are as one."

MAKING A PROPHET

"Everyone must have two pockets, with a note in each pocket, so that he or she can reach into one or the other, depending on the need. When feeling lowly and depressed, discouraged or disconsolate, one should reach into the right pocket, and there, find the words: Bishvili nivra ha-olam 'The world was created for me' (Sanhedrin 37B). But when feeling high and mighty, one should reach into the left pocket, and find the words: V'anokhi afar v'efer 'I am but dust and ashes' (Genesis 18:27)."

Rabbi Simcha Bunim

For those who thought Jews are just part of a quaint old belief system, one among many, or merely a social group, members of a heartwarming cultural club, they are about to have these illusions well and truly shattered. They would be surprised to discover that Jews are actually the heirs to a spiritual tradition of numerous illuminated prophets intimately connected to the Infinite, who taught various meditation techniques and consciousness-raising exercises that are still accessible to us today. One can learn more about this well-trodden path to enlightenment by reading this extract from Rabbi Alexander Seinfeld's *The Art of Amazement*:

"The very idea of Jewish spirituality astonishes many people, especially Jews. For most of us, Judaism amounts to a set of holidays and rituals like Hannukah, Passover, bar mitzvahs, and bagels with cream cheese and lox.

"Some people are vaguely aware of an esoteric Judaism, associated with certain texts such as the *Zohar*. Since most of these were published in the Middle Ages, there is an erroneous popular belief that Jewish mysticsm began then.

"In reality, meditative disciplines have been part of Judaism since ancient times. Ancient Israel abounded with meditation schools, teachers and disciples, especially during the First Temple era (ca. 900 – 500

B.C.E.). These schools were led by spiritual masters known as *nevi'im,* loosely translated as "prophets" but understood more precisely as masters of transcendental meditation.

"These masters promulgated many techniques, some of which fit our stereotypes and others do not. Miscellaneous examples include chanting, gazing at a flame, and breathing techniques. One of the advanced methods involves quietly concentrating on certain letters of the Hebrew alphabet. These meditative practices have survived the millennia, passed discreetly from teacher to student.

"In fact, this chain of tradition seems to have originated well before the First Temple period. For instance, the Bible says of Abraham's son Isaac:

> *Va'yeitzei Yitzchak lasuach ba'sadeh…*
> *Isaac went out to* lasuach *in the field…*
> GENESIS 24:63

"Biblical commentaries differ widely on the exact meaning of *lasuach,* which appears exclusively here. Some say it involves sitting still, others say it means walking, talking, or even singing. But nearly all commentaries agree that the term is an overt reference to a meditative practice.

"The Midrash supports this consensus. *Midrash* means "exposition" and pertains to a compendium of oral traditions that were committed to paper in the form of Biblical commentaries over most of the first millennium C.E. The Midrash contains many details of the stories that are obviously missing from the text of the Torah. For example, the Torah says explicitly that "Terah begat Abraham" (*Genesis 7:24*), yet never mentions Abraham's mother. Only from Midrash do we know her name to be Amasalai. Thus Midrash, often translated as "legends" or "tales," might be understood as the "footnotes" to the Biblical narrative. These Biblical footnotes give a context to Isaac's meditation. The Midrash relates that Abraham, Isaac, and Jacob were all steeped in even older wisdom received from Noah's son Shem. Jacob himself spent fourteen years in Shem's academy. This little-known story indicates the centrality of the contemplative arts to ancient Judaism.

"This woven fabric of wisdom and custom sprang from the initiative of one couple, Sarah and Abraham, who died in 1630 and 1592 B.C. E., respectively. In Jewish spirituality, Abraham was the central stalk from which the flower bloomed. He was a spiritual giant whose greatness can hardly be overstated. He independently discovered the art of amazement and its related spiritual principles. He and Sarah became great spiritual leaders (Abraham taught the men and Sarah the women). They were exceedingly wealthy and opened their tent "on all four sides" to welcome every stranger. The Midrash gives them a very noble image, like unofficial royalty of the Middle East.

"It is fascinating to note that Abraham and Sarah lived just before the original Aryans, whose immigration to India in 1500-1000 B.C.E. sparked the beginning of Vedic religion, which later spawned Hinduism, Buddhism, Sikhism, and others. Compare, for instance, the following names:

Abraham...Brahma
Sarah...Sarasvati

"Brahma is the higher god in Vedic mythology and Sarasvati is the primary of Brahma's two wives. In the Torah, Abraham also had two wives, and Sarah is the primary of the two. Does this coincidence point us to the destination of Abraham's children of his old age, whom he "sent eastward, to the land of the East, before he died" (*Genesis 25:6*)?

"From what we know of Abraham's stature as a teacher and leader, it is likely that his progeny became spiritual leaders in their own right. If some of them did reach the Indus valley, it is not hard to imagine them teaching the indigenous population a spiritual system that associates the names of Abraham and Sarah with transcendence itself. This brief background should intrigue the skeptic and reassure the seeker that

Jewish spirituality has the proper credentials to be a true foundation of transcendental wisdom.

When a person meditates on these things and recognizes all the creations – from forces, to constellations, to people like oneself – he will be in awe of the wisdom of the Hidden Source in all of its handiworks and all its creations. Pleasurable identification with the Infinite will increase, and one's soul will expand and body will strive to love the Infinite, the Source.

RABBI MOSES MAIMONIDES (RAMBAM) (1135 – 1204)

"Ancient Jews understood this role of meditation in spiritual growth with such clarity that meditation became as integral to ancient Israelite culture as television has become to ours. Jews learned meditation in schools all over ancient Israel. As meditation practices developed over the millennia, the ultimate goal has remained the same – to transcend one's consciousness beyond the mundane, finite here-and-now toward the infinite source of the mundane.

"The ancient meditation schools used a curriculum that was specifically tailored toward the achievement of a clear and direct line of communication with the Infinite. Such a level of communication is the ultimate state of transcendental awareness and is called *neviut*, or prophecy.

"Prophecy is generally misunderstood. It does not mean simply telling the future. A person who tells the future via naturalistic forces is called a fortune-teller or a soothsayer, an extremely un-Jewish practice, according to the Torah. Since the greatest Jews of history were prophets, they must have been doing something other than (or in addition to) predicting the future.

"Part of the misunderstanding of prophecy comes from the fact that the Bible records the prophecies of only forty-eight post-Mosaic prophets, many of whom bring tidings of doom and destruction. No wonder the word *prophet* has become associated with prescience.

"In fact, prophecy is defined by an experience rather than by a specific type of pronouncement. We actually know very little about the prophetic experience because true prophecy has been absent from the world since the fourth century B.C.E. Yet the scattered evidence, including descriptive sources, indicates an experience of channelling energy.

"To reach the prophetic state of consciousness required a long period of study, meditation and inner purification. To succeed required both tremendous self-discipline and professional guidance. Modern authorities like Rabbi Joseph Soloveitchik affirm that prophecy is the 'ultimate peak' of human creative achievement."

Speaking about the potential pitfalls and dangers that a spiritual aspirant needs to guard against when seeking the mystical experiences that lead to the acquisition of the gift of prophecy, Rabbi Aryeh Kaplan writes in *Meditation and the Bible:*

"One thing that we see clearly is that the forbidden idolatrous and occult practices very closely resembled the mystical practices of the prophets. This may have been one reason why the prophetic practices were concealed as hidden mysteries, restricted to very small societies. This was particularly true after the close of the prophetic period, where these practices were virtually unknown outside of very small, select circles.

"The prophets knew that many people who did not have the proper preparation or temperament would attempt to emulate these practices. When unsuccessful, these people would turn to the relatively simple but forbidden practices of the idolators. The prophetic methods were therefore shrouded in virtually absolute secrecy, and there is no express mention of them in the entire Bible.

"The Talmud states that during the prophetic period, there existed a literal 'lust for idolatry.' It may seem somewhat difficult to understand how people could have a lust for something like idolatry, which, according to the context, was as strong as the sexual desire. But when there were many people involved in the mystical experience, the desire to join them was very strong. The mystical experience is one of the sweetest, profoundest, most uplifting experiences possible, and is something that can be very greatly desired.

"At the same time, however, the true mystical experience is *Ruach HaKodesh* which can only be attained after one has completed the ten preliminary levels. Before one can reach this level he must literally be a saint, both in his relationship to God and his dealings with man. Beyond this, one could not even enter the prophetic schools until he had undergone years of discipline and purification. People were therefore tempted to take shortcuts, and among the most readily available were the occult practices of the idolators.

"During the time of Solomon's Temple, the Talmud informs us that there were millions of individuals involved in the prophetic mysteries. It is no coincidence that idolatry and sorcery were so prevalent at the time. People who could not reach the spiritual heights of the prophets took the easy way of idolatry and occultism instead. It is therefore no coincidence that when the prophetic schools were abolished after the destruction of Solomon's Temple, the 'lust for idolatry' was also nullified.

"Still there were small closed schools that kept the spirit of the prophets alive. In order to prevent the masses from once again turning to idolatrous practices as a substitute for true prophetic meditation, they restricted the spread of these ideas. Finally, outside of a small school, these practices were totally unknown. The only ones who had any idea of the methods was a small, restricted school of Kabbalists.

"Maimonides writes that prophecy will have to be restored before the coming of the Messiah. As we have seen, however, prophecy does not occur automatically, but must be cultivated with extensive discipline through very specific practices. Before the Messianic age, therefore, these practices will have to be revealed and taught. Only then will there be a fulfilment of the prophecy, where God said, 'After that, I will pour out My spirit on all flesh, and your sons and daughters will prophesy. Your old men will dream dreams, and your young men will see visions' (*Joel 3:1*).

"As for the thought and meditation – that are in the brain, and the power of speech – engaged in the words of Torah – that is in the mouth, these being the innermost garment of the divine soul, not to mention the divine soul itself which is clothed in them – all of them are completely merged in perfect unity with the Supreme Will, and are not merely a vehicle. For the Supreme Will is identical with the very subject of the halachah wherein one thinks and speaks, inasmuch as all the laws are particular streams flowing from the inner Supreme Will itself, since His blessed Will willed it that a particular act be permissible, or a food ritually fit for consumption, or this [person] inculpable and that entirely innocent, or the reverse. So also are the letter combinations of the Pentateuch, Prophets and Hagiographa a promulgation of His will and wisdom which are united with the blessed En Sof in perfect unity, since He is the Knower and the Knowledge, and so forth. This then is the meaning of the above mentioned quotation that 'The Torah and the Holy One blessed be He, are altogether One,' and not merely 'organs' of the King, as are the commandments."

SOULFULNESS
Rabbi Aryeh Kaplan on Meditation

It is universally accepted by the Kabbalists that the first ones to engage in these meditative methods were the patriarchs and prophets, who used them to attain enlightenment and prophecy. Although there are many allusions to this in the Bible, the scripture is virtually silent when it comes to providing explicit descriptions of their methods. Still if one looks at the appropriate texts, one can gain considerable insight into the methods that were in use in the time of the prophets.

The earliest direct statement regarding method comes from the First Century, from the early Talmudic period. Here we find some of the greatest Talmudists engaged in the mystical arts, making use of a number of meditative techniques to attain spiritual elevation and ascend to the transcendental realm. Many of these techniques consisted of the repetition of divine names, as well as intense concentration on the transcendental spheres. What little we know of their methods is preserved in a few fragments, as well in a remarkable complete text, *Hekhalot Rabatai* (The Greater Chambers), of which the main parts are presented for the first time in translation in this book (*Meditation and Kabbalah*).

It was during this period that some of the main classics of Kabbalah were written. These include the *Sefer Yetzirah* (Book of Formation), the Bahir and the Zohar. These involved even higher levels than those described in the *Hekhalot,* and for the most part, only the barest hints are provided as to how these levels were reached.

With the close of the Talmudic period, these methods became restricted to a few very small closed secret societies. Both the Bahir and the Zohar remained completely unknown outside of these societies, and were not revealed until the late Twelfth and Thirteenth Centuries respectively. The publication of the Bahir in particular gave impetus to the study of the mysteries, and a number of individuals began to openly teach the secret methods.

Most remarkable among these was Rabbi Abraham Abulafia (1240-1295). Having received the tradition from earlier sources, he was the first to actually put them in writing. For this, he was condemned in many circles, although most Kabbalists consider his methods to be authentic and based on a reliable tradition. Several of his contemporaries, most notably, Rabbi Isaac of Acco and Rabbi Joseph Gikatalia, also speak of meditative methods.

Most of their work, however, was eclipsed by the publication of the Zohar in the middle 1290's. This great classic gripped the imagination of almost all Kabbalists of the time, and the teachings of other schools was virtually forgotten. It is therefore no accident that many books written before this were never published, and among those which have not been lost, a good number exist only in manuscript.

Since the Zohar has little to say about meditative methods, many important Kabbalists began to ignore the subject completely. They were too involved in trying to unravel the mysteries of this ancient book that had been concealed for many centuries. There were a few exceptions, however, and these Kabbalists made use of the methods of Abulafia, Gikatalia and Isaac of Acco. For over two hundred years, however, we find virtually nobody exploring the Zohar itself to ascertain the meditative methods used by its authors.

The main attempts in this direction occurred in the Safed School which flourished during the Sixteenth Century. It reached its zenith in the teachings of Rabbi Isaac Luria (1534-1572), commonly known as the Ari, who showed how the various letter combinations found in the Zohar were actually meant to be used as meditative devices. Although the Ari wrote almost nothing himself, his teachings were arduously copied by his disciples, and fill almost two dozen large volumes. To a large extent, all this was an introduction to the methodology involved in his system of meditation.

Just as the Zohar had overshadowed everything when it was published, so did the writings of the Ari overwhelm the other schools three centuries later. His teachings were seen as the ultimate expression of the Kabbalah, and for the next two hundred years, the greatest part of Kabbalah literature devoted itself to their interpretation. Although the Ari's meditative methods were used by a few individuals, and possibly by one or two minor schools, for the most part the Kabbalists devoted themselves to theory rather than practice.

The next great renascence came with the rise of the Hasidic movement, founded by Rabbi Israel, the Baal Shem Tov (1698-1760). When their works are studied, it becomes obvious that the Baal Shem and his closest disciples were ardent students of the earlier meditative texts of the Kabbalah, and in the Hasidic classics, these texts are often paraphrased.

During the second half of the Eighteenth Century, and perhaps the first decade or two of the Nineteenth, many people engaged in the classical meditative techniques of Kabbalah, often describing the high spiritual states that they attained.

The opposition to this, especially where it involved teaching these methods to the masses, was very strong. An entire group, known as the *Mitnagdim* (opposers), arose to combat the Hasidim, vigorously denouncing their methods. As a result, the Hasidim themselves began to de-emphasise their meditative practices, and eventually these were virtually forgotten.

(One) type of meditation is that which is non-directed. Such meditation strives for a stillness of the mind and a withdrawal from all perception, both internal and external. It plays an important role in the advanced states of many other methods, but at the same time, it can also be used as a method in its own right. Very little is expressly written about this method, but it appears to play a role in the teachings of such Hasidic masters as Rabbi Dov Ber, the Maggid of Mezeritch (1704-1772) and Rabbi Levi Yitzchak of Berdichev (1740-1809).

There is evidence that this method was used, at least for the most advanced, in the very terminology of the Kabbalah. Indeed, in a number of cases, it is only when looked upon in this sense that some terminology is comprehensible. Thus, for example, the Kabbalists call the highest level of transcendence *Ayin,* literally "Nothingness". Actually, this alludes to the ultimate level reached by non-directed meditation, where all perception and imagery cease to exist.

There is one word that is consistently used as a term for meditation by the commentators, philosophers and Kabbalists. The word which most often denotes meditation is *Hitbodedut*. The verb, "to meditate", is represented by the word *Hitboded.*

The word *Hitboded* is derived from the root *Badad*, meaning "to be secluded". Literally, then, *Hitbodedut* actually means self isolation, and in some cases, actually refers to nothing more than physical seclusion and isolation. In many other places, however, it is used to denote a state of consciousness involving the isolation of the self, that is, the isolation of the individual's most basic essence.

Thus, when discussed in a Kabbalistic context, the word *Hitbodedut* means much more than mere physical isolation. It refers to a state of internal isolation, where the individual mentally secludes his essence from his thoughts. One of the greatest Kabbalists, Rabbi Chaim Vital (1543-1620), often speaks of such mental seclusion, saying that "one must seclude himself *(hitboded)* in his thoughts to the ultimate degree". In doing this, one separates his soul from his body to such a degree that he no longer feels any relationship to his physical self. The soul is thus isolated, and as Rabbi Chaim Vital concludes, "the more one separates himself from the physical, the greater will be his enlightenment".

This state of mental seclusion is very important to the prophetic experience. The clearest description of this state is presented by Rabbi Levi ben Gershon (1288-1344), a major Jewish philosopher; often known as Gersonides, or simply by the acrostic, "the Ralbag". He writes that the attainment of prophetic revelation "requires the isolation *(hitbodedut)* of the consciousness from the imagination, or both of these from the other perceptive mental faculties".

Rabbi Isaac of Acco also uses the same definition. Speaking of individuals seeking prophecy, he writes, "They fulfil the conditions of meditation *(Hitbodedut)* which has the effect of nullifying the senses and divorcing the thought processes of the soul from all perception, clothing it in the spiritual essence of the transcendental".

One of the clearest expressions of this has been developed by Rabbi Abraham Maimonides (1186-1237), son of the famed Moses Maimonides. He writes that there are two different types of self isolation

29

(hitbodedut), external and internal. External *hitbodedut* is nothing more than physical isolation, and this is usually desirable when one wishes to meditate. Internal *hitbodedut,* on the other hand, consists of isolating the soul from the perceptive faculty. When the mind is completely hushed in this manner, one becomes able to perceive the spiritual realm.

The word *Hitbodedut* therefore primarily is used to denote the isolation of the soul or ego from all external and internal stimuli. Any method or practice that is used to accomplish this is also called *Hitbodedut.* Since these are the practices that are usually referred to as "meditation", this is how the word *Hitbodedut* should be translated.

The best time for the deepest levels of meditation is in old age, when the intellect is well developed and the pull of the body is weak. Although young people may try to enter the mysteries, Abulafia taught that they will not reach the higher levels until they are advanced in age. This reflects the Talmudic teaching that such mysteries should not be taught to an individual unless he is "halfway through his years".

Highly controversial was Abulafia's claim to have attained true prophecy, even though he did not live in the Holy Land. According to the Midrash, prophecy can only be attained in the Holy Land, and not any place else, except under sharply restricted conditions. Abulafia refused to accept this literally, and said that the Holy Land discussed in this teaching referred to a specific spiritual level. If an individual reached this level, he could attain prophecy, no matter what his geographical location.

One of Rabbi Isaac of Acco's important teachings involves *Hishtavut,* a term derived from the root *shava,* meaning "equal". The term denotes making all things equal for oneself, and can be translated as equanimity, or more accurately, as stoicism. It involves total indifference to all outside influences good or bad. This is seen by Rabbi Isaac as a prerequisite for any true level of meditation, an idea that is mentioned by Abulafia, and discussed at length by Albotini.

The idea of *Hishtavut* is also found in earlier, non-Kabbalistic sources, the earliest beng *Chovot HaLevavot* (Duties of the Heart), by Rabbi Bachya ibn Pakuda (1050-1120). Actually, however, this concept is also found in the Talmud, where it is called "overcoming one's [natural] tendencies." Thus, the Talmud relates that the great mystic, Rabbi Nehunia ben HaKana, the central figure of the *Hekhalot*, said that this was one of the main traits responsible for his attainments. The Talmud also teaches that the mysteries involving the Name of Forty-Two can only be given over to one who has attained this level of stoicism. In another place, the Talmud speaks of prayer being answered immediately in a mystical manner, and again states that the reason was because the individual leading the prayers had been able to "overcome his tendencies".

The Talmud clearly states that those who attain this level of stoicism are able to radiate spiritually. It teaches, "Regarding those who are insulted but do not insult, who hear themselves scorned, but do not respond, who serve [God] with love and rejoice in suffering, it is written, 'Those who love [God] shall be like the sun, when it shines forth with [all] its strength' (Judges 5:31)".

This teaching had a profound effect on later Kabbalists. It is discussed at length in *Sulam HaAliyah* (Ladder of Ascent), and Isaac of Acco's primary teaching regarding this is quoted in its entirety in the unpublished Fourth Part of Rabbi Chaim Vital's *Shaarey Kedushah*. A similar idea was taught to Rabbi Joseph Caro by his angelic teacher.

It is significant to see that this very same idea is also found in early Hasidic teachings. The Baal Shem Tov, founder of the Hasidic movement, speaks at length regarding *Hishtavut*-stoicism and states that this is the intent of the verse usually translated as, "I have set *(shivi-ti)* God before me at all times" (Psalms 16:8). According to the Baal Shem, the word *shivi-ti*, instead of being translated, "I have set," should be translated, "I have been stoic". The verse then reads, "I have been stoic, God is before me at all times".

At first this interpretation may seem far-fetched to Bible scholars, but actually, it makes a number of other very difficult verses much more understandable. Thus, instead of, "I have placed *(shivi-ti)* and have quieted my soul" (Psalms 131:1), we can now read this verse, "I have become stoic and have quieted my soul. "Another verse where this interpretation fits well is, "I have chosen a path of faith, through Your judgments I have become stoic" (Psalms 119:30). The same is true of the verse in Isaiah, "I made myself stoic *(shivi-ti)* like a lion until morning"

(Isaiah 38:13). In all these verses, it would be very difficult to translate *Shivi-ti* as "I have placed".

In a number of places, Rabbi Isaac speaks of *Mitbodedim* or "meditators" as if there were regular organized groups of these individuals. The very fact that so many Kabbalistic schools contemporary to him speak of various meditative techniques also seems to support this. In a number of places, he also speaks of the science of letter combination (tzeruf) citing this as an important means for attaining enlightenment.

Rabbi Isaac of Acco wrote a number of books, none of which were ever published, except for fragments in scholarly journals. His best known work is *Meirat Eynayim* (Light of the Eyes), a commentary on the Torah explaining the teachings of the Ramban. Another important Kabbalistic work is his *Otzar Chaim* (Treasury of Life), which consists mostly of mysteries revealed to him while in a meditative state. He also wrote commentaries on *Sefer Yetzirah,* and *Pirkey Rabbi Eliezer,* an ancient Midrash. Parts of these have been published in journals.

Highly significant is his autobiographical *Divrey Yamim* (Chronicles), which he mentions in his *Otzar Chaim,* but no manuscript of this exists. Also mentioned there is another work, *Chaim DeOraita* (Life of the Torah), which is not noted by historians, but may be the mystical unknown book of his that is occasionally quoted by the Kabbalists.

TEACHINGS
I, the insignificant Isaac, son of Solomon, of Acco, proclaim this both to individuals and the masses, who wish to know the mystery of binding one's soul on high.

One can attach his thoughts to God, and when one does so consistently, there is no question that he will be worthy of the World to Come ~ and God's Name will be with him constantly, both in this world and in the next.

The Tetragrammaton in Ashurit Script

יהוה

You should constantly keep the letters of the Unique Name in your mind as if they were in front of you, written in a book with Torah (Ashurit) script. Each letter should appear infinitely large.

When you depict the letters of the Unique Name in this manner, your mind's eye should gaze on them, and at the same time, your heart should be directed toward the Infinite Being (Ain Sof). Your gazing and thought should be as one.

This is the mystery of true attachment, regarding which the Torah says, "To Him you shall attach yourself" (Deuteronomy 10:20).

[If you are able to do this,] no evil will befall you, you will not be subject to errors caused by logic or emotion, and you will not be the victim of accidents. As long as you are attached to God, you are above all accidents, and are in control of events.

You must respect God, and be careful not to attach your thoughts to Him when you are not in a clean place. Do not do so in filthy alleys, when your hands are not clean, or when you are in the presence of idols.

I heard the following from a pious sage who had served Rabbi Isaac [the Blind), son of the Raavad (Rabbi Abraham ben David of Posquieres, 1120-1198):

[Rabbi Isaac] had been born blind, and had never seen with his physical eyes. Whenever he would go any place, he would tell his attendant, "When we pass by a place of idolatry, quicken your pace as much as you can".

It appears to me that this was done for the glory of God. His thoughts were always bound to God, and because of the unclean spirit that dwells in the idols, he could not think such thoughts [while in proximity to them]. This was a place of ultimate uncleanness, while his thoughts were on the Root of ultimate holiness. He would therefore hurry away from there, so that he could return to his normal state of mind.

You may ask why one should bind his thoughts to the Tetragrammaton more than any other name. The reason is that this Name is the cause of causes and the source of all sources. Included in it are all things, from Keter-Crown (the highest Sefirah) to the lowliest gnat. Blessed be the Name of the glory of His kingdom forever and ever.

It is regarding this name that the Psalmist said, "I have placed YHVH before me at all times" (Psalms 16:8). This alludes to what we have said, that his eyes and heart were always directed toward God, and it is as if the Name (YHVH) was written before him ...

When an individual is worthy of the mystery of Attachment *(Devekut),* he can also be worthy of the mystery of Stoicism *(Hishtavut).* After he is worthy of Stoicism, he can also be worthy of Meditation *(Hitbodedut).* And after he is worthy of Meditation, he can be worthy of *Ruach HaKodesh* (Holy Spirit, enlightenment). From there, he can reach the level of Prophecy, where he can actually predict the future.

In explaining the mystery of Stoicism, Rabbi Abner related the following account:

A sage once came to one of the Meditators *(Mitbodedim)* and asked that he be accepted into their society. The other replied, "My son, blessed are you to God. Your intentions are good. But tell me, have you attained stoicism or not?" The sage said, "Master, explain your words." The Meditator said, "If one man is praising you and another is insulting you, are the two equal in your eyes or not?" He replied, "No my master. I have pleasure from those who praise me, and pain from those who degrade me. But I do not take revenge or bear a grudge".

The other said, "Go in peace my son. You have not attained stoicism. You have not reached a level where your soul does not feel the praise of one who honors you, nor the degradation of one who insults you. You are not prepared for your thoughts to be bound up on high, that you should come and meditate *(hitboded)*. Go and increase the humbleness of your heart, and learn to treat everything equally until you've become stoic. Only then will you be able to meditate.

Light of the Eyes.

One who is worthy to reach the level of meditation *(hitbodedut)* has peace in this life. To reach this level, one must bind himself to three traits, and keep himself from their opposite. He will then have peace in this world, and certainly in the next.

These are the three traits: One must rejoice in his portion, he must love meditation, and he must flee from position and honor. This involves the subjugation of the heart.

Rabbi Isaac of Acco writes in the name of Rabbi Moshe, a disciple of Rabbi Joseph Gikatalia :
If a person's heart impels him to rectify his traits, perfecting his personality and deeds, he should pursue humility to the ultimate degree. He should "be insulted but not insult, hear himself scorned but not respond". The Divine Presence will then immediately rest on him and he will not have to learn from any mortal being, for the spirit of God will teach him.

Elsewhere, [Rabbi Isaac of Acco] writes :
We found this in the books of the Kabbalists who were worthy of the way of truth:
One of the great rectifications for one who wishes to know God is that he should be among those who are "insulted but does not insult". This should even be true with regard to people of whom he is not afraid and before whom he has no shame, such as his wife and children. Even if members of his household insult him, he should not answer, except to correct their ways . . . . But inwardly, he should feel no anger, but his

35

heart should always be joyful, attached [to God] no matter what happens.

PARALLELS

It is related that one of the Hasidim asked one of his companions, "Have you attained stoicism *(hishtavutl)?"* When the other asked the meaning of his question, he explained," Have you [reached a level where] praise and insult are equal in your eyes?" The other replied negatively, and he said, "If this is true, then you have not reached the [necessary level]. Continue to strive in this direction, and you may be able to reach this level. It is the highest level of piety and its desired end".

Rabbi Bachya ibn Pekudah (1050-1120).

[My angelic master taught me this:] Do not worry about anything in the world, other than that which will influence your worship of God. With regard to worldly things, everything should be the same as its opposite. This is the mystery of the words of the sage, who asked an initiate who wished to involve himself in Unifications *(Yichudim)*, "Have you attained stoicism?" If a person does not see that all good in the physical world is exactly the same as its evil, it is impossible for him to Unify all things.

Rabbi Joseph Caro (1488-1575).

"I have been stoic, God is before me at all times." (Psalms 16:8). This denotes a level of stoicism with regard to all that befalls a person. Whether people insult him or praise him, it should all be equal. The same is true of eating, whether he eats sweetmeats or gall, it should all be equal to him. In this manner, one can dispel the Evil Urge *(Yetzer HaRa)* completely.

Rabbi Israel Baal Shem Tov (1698-1760).

It is told that one of the Hasidim was once asked, "What was the happiest occasion in your life?" He told the following story:
I was once travelling on a ship along with merchants carrying costly goods. I wished to meditate *(hitboded)* on my Creator, and I went down into the bowels of the ship, lying there in the lowest place. The young son of one of the merchants stood himself over me, insulting me and spitting in my face. He then uncovered himself and urinated on me. I was astounded at his brazenness.

But as God lives, my soul was not downcast as a result of this. After he left, I was exceedingly happy, realizing that my soul had reached a level of true humility. I realize that through this trait, one can "walk among the Ones who stand". This trait dominated me so much that I felt absolutely nothing whatsoever.

Rabbi Eliahu di Vidas (16th Century).

The (Baal Shem Tov's) Epistle

On Rosh HaShanah 5507 (September 15, 1746), I made an oath and elevated my soul in the manner known to you. I saw things that I had never before witnessed since the day I was born. The things that I learned and saw there could not be communicated, even if I would be able to speak to you in person.

When I returned to the lower Garden of Eden, I saw innumerable souls, both living and dead, some whom I knew and others whom I did not. They were fleeting back and forth, going from one universe to another through the Column that is known to those who delve in mysteries. They were in a state of joy that was so great that the lips cannot express it, and the physical ear is too gross to hear about it.

There were also many wicked people who were repenting, and their sins were forgiven since this was a special time of grace. Even to my eyes it was wondrous how many were accepted as penitents, many of whom you know. There was great joy among them, too, and they also ascended in the above-mentioned manner.

All of them beseeched and petitioned me unceasingly: "Go higher with the glory of your Torah. May God grant you greater understanding to perceive and know these things. Ascend with us, so that you can be our help and support."

Because of the great joy that I saw among them, I decided to ascend with them. Due to the great danger involved in ascending to the supernal Universes, I asked my Master to come with me. From the time that I began, I had never before ascended to such a high level. Step by step I ascended until I entered the chamber of the Messiah. There the Messiah studies Torah with all the sages and saints, as well as with the Seven Shepherds.

I saw great joy there, but I did not know the reason for it. At first I thought that the reason for this joy was that I had passed away from the physical world, heaven forbid. Later, they told me that I had not died, since they have great pleasure on high when I bring about Unifications through the holy Torah down below. But to this very day, I do not know the reason for that joy.

I spoke to the Messiah himself and asked him, "When is your majesty coming?" He replied, "This shall be your sign. It will be at a time when your teachings become widespread in the world, and 'your springs overflow.'

"It will be when the things which I have taught you, and which you have yourself perceived, become known, so that others can also bring about Unifications and elevate themselves like you do. All the Husks will then be annihilated, and it will be a time of grace and salvation".

I was *very* surprised, and distressed, since it would take a long time for this to be possible. But when I was there, I learned three specific remedies and three holy Names, and they are easy to learn and explain.

My mind was then set at ease, and I realized that it would be possible for people in my generation to reach the same level and state as I did. They would then be able to ascend, learn and perceive, just like myself. All during my lifetime, I was not granted permission to reveal this.

For your sake, I made a request that I might be allowed to teach this to you, but permission was denied. I am still bound by this oath, but this I can tell you, and let God be your help:

Let your path be toward God. When you pray and study let [my words] not forsake you. With every word and expression that leaves your lips, have in mind to bring about a Unification. Every single letter contains universes, souls and godliness, and as they ascend, one becomes bound to the other and they become unified. The letters then become unified and attached to form a word. They are then actually unified with the Divine Essence, and in all these aspects, your soul is included with them.

All universes are then unified as one, and immeasurable joy and delight results. Consider the joy of a bridegroom and bride in this lowly physical world, and you will understand how great is this delight. God will certainly help you. Wherever you turn you will succeed and prosper. "Give wisdom to the wise, and he will become still wiser."

MEDITATION

An important part of the Baal Shem Tov's teachings involved Hitbodedut meditation. This was an integral part of his personal life as well, and it is reported that, as a young child, he would miss his lessons, going off to meditate *(hitboded)* in the forests . During his seven years of seclusion, he would meditate in the mountains, as well as in a special cave. When he studied together with the son of Rabbi Adam, he did so in a special "Meditation Room" *(Beit Hitbodedut),* and it was in this room that they engaged in meditation in an attempt to commune with the Angel of the Torah. Later, when he was a famed leader, he would also spend much time in such a "Meditation Room."

Most of the Baal Shem Tov's general teachings regarding meditation are found in the writings of his greatest disciple, Rabbi Dov Ber, the Mezeritcher Maggid. A few of these are also included in the Baal Shem's ethical will:

In our generations, we have limited intelligence and must strengthen our love and reverence of God. In your mind, you must therefore constantly meditate *(hitboded)* on the love and reverence of God. Even when you are studying, it is good to pause occasionally and to meditate in your mind. This is true even though it may take time from your sacred studies. In your mind, constantly meditate *(hitboded)* on the Divine Presence. Have no other thought in your mind other than your love, seeking that [the Divine Presence] should bind itself to you. Constantly repeat in your mind, "When will I be worthy for the light of the Divine Presence to dwell with me."

You can lie in bed and appear to be sleeping, but at that time, you can actually be meditating *(hitboded)* upon God,

When you wish to enter a [high] state of meditation *(hitbodedut),* you should have someone else with you. When a person does this while alone, he can be in great danger. Two people should therefore be together, and one should meditate, [mentally secluded] with his Creator.

STATES OF CONSCIOUSNESS

Although the earlier meditative Kabbalists occasionally discuss their experiences, they provide very little theory regarding states of consciousness. One of the first to speak specifically of states of consciousness appears to be the Baal Shem Tov.

The two states of consciousness that he discusses are *Mochin DeGadlut* and *Mochin DeKatnut,* or more commonly, simply *Gadlut* and *Katnut.*

These terms are somewhat difficult to translate. The word *Mochin* literally means "brains," and in the Ari's terminology, refers to "mentalities". In the context used by the Baal Shem, however, the term *Mochin* actually should be translated, "states of consciousness."

Gadlut means "maturity" or "greatness," while *Katnut* means "immaturity" or "smallness." Actually, then, the best way to translate *Mochin DeGadlut* would be "expanded consciousness", while *Mochin DeKatnut* would be "constricted consciousness". Within the general theory of meditation, it is known that an important goal of this practice is to bring a person to a state of expanded consciousness.

These are actually borrowed terms. When the Ari speaks of the Partzuf of Zer Anpin, he expands upon its development which is outlined in the most mysterious Zoharic texts, the Greater and Lesser *Idras.* In its development, the Partzuf of Zer Anpin goes through stages of birth and growth. Like a human being, this Partzuf can thus be in a state of immaturity, as well as one of maturity. The immature state is called *Katnut,* while that of maturity is called *Gadlut.*

As the Partzuf matures, so does its mentalities. It is in this context that we find the terms *Mochin DeKatnut* and *Mochin DeGadlut,* in their original meaning. *Mochin DeKatnut* denotes the immature mentalities of Zer Anpin, while *Mochin DeGadlut* denotes the mature mentalities.

This anthropomorphism is to be taken symbolically rather than literally, and the states of immaturity and maturity do not exist in different time spans. Both states exist at all times, and are responsible for different effects in the lower world. The Ari expresses it in this manner:

"The power of forgetfulness in man is a result of these Immature Mentalities *(Mochin DeKatnut)*. One must transmit Mature Mentalities *(Mochin DeGadlut)* [to Zer Anpin]. When this is accomplished through one's deeds, he causes [the Immature Mentalities] to descend to [the Female Partzuf. The Immature Mentalities which are derived from the name] Elokim is thus expelled and removed completely from Zer Anpin. If a person can do this, he will then have a wondrous memory, and will comprehend all the mysteries of the Torah".

Since Zer Anpin is the "Supernal Man", everything in this Partzuf also has a counterpart in man. The Baal Shem Tov therefore taught that these states of immaturity and maturity in Zer Anpin parallel different states of consciousness in the human mind. In man these are the states of expanded and constricted consciousness.

When a person is in a state of expanded consciousness, he is enlightened in all walks of life. He has realized the vanity of the mundane world and the greatness of the spiritual. Everything that he does is with a different awareness, whether it is eating and drinking, worship or study. The idea is discussed often in the teachings of the Baal Shem Tov.

"Sometimes you can speak on high with your soul alone, without your body. This is when you separate yourself from your body, and it is called "divestment of the physical" *(Hit-pashtut HaGashmiut)*. In such a state you feel no bodily sensation and are totally unaware of the physical world.

"When you are properly attached to God, you can engage in any activity that you wish. It appears that you are gazing at the subject of your activity, but actually, you are gazing at nothing other than God. "I heard this from my master [The Baal Shem Tov]. Wherever a person places his thoughts, that is where all of him is.

"Wherever you ascend on high, keep in mind that you are bringing yourself closer to God, and binding yourself to Him on a higher level.

"At all times during the day, even when you are not praying, you should mentally elevate your thoughts on high. This takes great effort. Strengthen yourself with all your power of concentration, even if at first you do not ascend very high.

"Faith is all-important. Many people love and fear God, but still, they accomplish nothing on high because they lack absolute faith."

In classical meditation, the most difficult path is undirected meditation. This is a path where one must totally clear one's mind of all thought and sensation, whether physical or spiritual. All that one experiences on this level is absolute nothingness.

Prior to the Hasidic masters, there is virtually no mention whatsoever of this method. Even in the Hasidic writings, it is only mentioned occasionally and obliquely, but the few references are highly significant. It is discussed most often by the Mezeritcher Maggid, and by his most illustrious disciple, Rabbi Levi Yitzchak of Berdichev (1740 - 1809).

SOURCES

The many levels of the mind include the thinker, thought and speech. One is influenced by the other.

Speech exists in time. Thought is also in time, since a person has different thoughts at different times.

There is also an essence that binds the thinker to thought. This is an essence that cannot be grasped. It is the attribute of Nothingness. It is often referred to as the Hyle [the state between potential and realization].

An egg becomes a chicken. There is, however, an instant when it is neither chicken nor egg. No person can determine that instant, for in that instant, it is a state of Nothingness.

The same is true of the transition of thinker to thought, or of thought to speech. It is impossible to grasp the essence that unites them. In order to bind them all together, one must reach the level of Nothingness.

Moses thus said, "If Nothingness, erase me" (Exodus 32:32). [The Israelites had bowed down to the Golden Calf and] had been blemished by idolatry. What Moses wanted to do was elevate them back to their original level. He therefore brought himself to the level of Nothingness, and [wishing to go still higher,] he prayed, "erase me". When he reached the highest level, he was able to bind all things on high.

Think of yourself as nothing, and totally forget yourself when you pray. Only have in mind that you are praying for the Divine Presence. You can then enter the Universe of Thought, a state that is beyond time. Everything in this realm is the same, life and death, land and sea.

... But in order to enter the Universe of Thought where all is the same, you must relinquish your ego, and forget all your troubles. You cannot reach this level if you attach yourself to physical worldly things. For then, you are attached to the division between good and evil, which is included in the seven days of creation. How then can you approach a level above time, where absolute unity reigns.

Furthermore, if you consider yourself as "something", and ask for your own needs, then God cannot clothe Himself in you. God is infinite, and no vessel can hold Him at all, except when a person makes himself like Nothing.

God is boundless. This means that there is nothing physical that can hinder His presence. He fills every element of space in all universes that He created, on all levels, and there is no place devoid of Him.

When a person ascends from one level to the next, but still wants to attain more, then he has no limits and is literally like the Infinite. This person then has the attribute with which to grasp the seed transmitted from the Infinite Being.

But when a person says, "That which I can grasp is sufficient for me", he then only aspires to the straw and chaff, which are the Husks.

Man is primarily his mind. It would be natural for something which is mind to only bind itself to mental concepts.

One should therefore keep in mind this thought: "Why should I use my mind to think about physical things? When I do this I lower my mind by binding it to a lower level. It would be better for me to elevate my mind to the highest level, by binding my thoughts to the Infinite." Even physical things must serve the Creator in a spiritual manner.

It is thus taught, "They are My slaves, and not slaves of slaves." Love is not restricted by limitations. For love does not have any bounds, being an aspect of the Infinite love.

If one has love for something physical, then this physical thing becomes a vessel [that limits] his love. But when one has love for the Infinite Being, then his love is clothed in the Infinite. Both the love and its vessel are then boundless. The same is true of all other attributes. [God is called] the Endless One *(Ain Sof)*, and not the Beginningless One.

If He were called the Beginningless One, it would be impossible to even begin to speak about Him. But to some extent, it is possible to comprehend Him through His creation. This is a beginning, but it has no end.

Rabbi Levi Yitzchak:

The most important thing to realize is that God created all and that He is all. God's influence never ceases. At every instant, He gives existence to His creation, to all the universes, to the heavenly chambers, and to all the angels....

We therefore say [in the prayer before the *Sh'ma)*, "He *forms* light and creates darkness" [in the present tense), and not "He *formed* light and created darkness" [in the past tense]. We say that God "creates" in the present tense because every second he creates and gives existence to all that is.

Everything comes from God. He is perfect and He includes all things. When a person attains the attribute of Nothingness, he realizes that he is nothing, and that God is giving him existence. He can then say that God "creates" - in the present tense. This means that God is creating, even at this very moment.

When a person looks at himself and not at Nothingness, then he is on a level of "somethingness" [and independent existence]. He then says that God "created" - in the past tense. This means that God created him earlier [but that he now has independent existence]. We therefore say the blessing, "[Blessed are You, O God ...] who *created* man with wisdom." [We use the past tense,] since Wisdom is on a level of "somethingness."

We therefore find in the writings of the Ari that the expression, "God is King", is an aspect of Nothingness. For when we say that "God is King" [in the present tense] it means that He is presently giving us existence. This is the aspect of Nothingness - we are nothing, and it is God who is giving us the power [to exist].

On the level of Nothingness, everything is above the laws of nature. On the level of "somethingness", on the other hand, all things are bound by nature.

The way in which we bind "somethingness" to Nothingness is through the Torah and commandments. This is the meaning of the verse, "The Living Angels ran and returned" (Ezekiel 1:14) – [that is, from a level of Nothingness to one of "somethingness."]

The Zohar teaches that the commandments and Torah are both hidden and revealed. "Hidden" alludes to Nothingness, while "revealed" applies to "somethingness." They thus bind something to Nothingness, and Nothingness to somethingness.

This is the meaning of the word *Mitzvah*, meaning "commandment". When we reverse the Hebrew alphabet through the Atbash cipher, then Alef becomes Tav, Bet becomes Shin, and so on. Through this cipher, the Mem of *Mitzvah* becomes a Yod, while the Tzadi becomes a Heh.

The first two letters of *Mitzvah* [therefore] are Yod Heh, the first two letters of the Tetragrammaton, YHVH.

This is an aspect of Nothingness.

The last two letters of the word of *Mitzvah* are Vav Heh, (the last two letters of the Tetragrammaton).

This is an aspect of somethingness.

The letters Yod Heh in the word *Mitzvah* are hidden, just like the concept of Nothingness. [The letters Vav Heh, on the other hand, are written directly, and are revealed, just like somethingness.]

The commandments thus have a hidden part and a revealed part. The hidden part is our bringing pleasure to God through our observance of the commandments, since we have no way of detecting this. The revealed part is when we benefit ourselves, since this is visible.

This is the meaning of the verse, "Hidden things belong to the Lord our God, [but revealed things belong to us and to our children forever]" (Deuteronomy 34:22).

"Hidden things" allude to the hidden part of the commandment, and these "belong to the Lord our God." What we accomplish with relation to God is hidden from us.

"Revealed things belong to us and to our children," however, since the divine influence that we bring about is revealed to us.

***

At every instant, all universes receive sustenance and Life Force from God. Man, however, is the one who *motivates* this sustenance and transmits it to all worlds.

When a person wants to bring new sustenance to all universes, he must attach himself to the level of Nothingness. This is the level in all universes that were not constricted.

When man nullifies himself completely and attaches his thoughts to Nothingness, then a new sustenance flows to all universes. This is a sustenance that did not exist previously.

A person must fear God so much that his ego is totally nullified. Only then can he attach himself to Nothingness. Sustenance, filled with all good, then flows to all universes ....

The individual thus attaches the Life Force of all universes to Nothingness, which is higher than all worlds. ... On the level where this [Life Force] had not yet been constricted into the universes, it is attached to the Nothingness, which is called the Hyle. ...

***

46

Although Rabbi Nachman's teachings comprise a good number of volumes, his ideas regarding meditation are collected in a remarkable book called *Hishtapchut HaNefesh* (Outpouring of the Soul):

You must include yourself in God's unity, which is the imperative Existence. You cannot be worthy of this, however, unless you first nullify yourself. It is impossible to nullify yourself, however, without *Hitbodedut*-meditation.

When you meditate and express your spontaneous thoughts before God, you can be worthy of nullifying all desires and all evil traits. You will then be able to nullify your entire physical being, and become included in your Root.

The main time to meditate is at night. This is a time when the world is free from mundane concerns. Since people are involved in the mundane by day, you will be held back and confused, so that you will not be able to attach yourself to God and include yourself in Him. Even if you yourself are not so involved, since the world is concerned with worldly vanities, it is difficult for you to nullify yourself.

It is also necessary that you meditate in an isolated place. It should be outside the city, or on a lonely street, or some other place where other people are not found. For wherever people are found, they are involved in the mundane world. Even though they may not be in this place at that time, the very fact that they are usually there can confuse one's meditation, and then one cannot nullify himself and include himself in God.

You must therefore be alone, at night, on an isolated path, where people are not usually found. Go there and meditate, cleansing your heart and mind of all worldly affairs. You will then be worthy of a true aspect of self-nullification.

Meditating at night in an isolated place, you should make use of many prayers and thoughts, until you nullify one trait or desire. Then make use of much meditation to nullify another trait or desire.

Continue in such a time and place, proceeding in this manner, until you have nullified all. If some ego remains, work to nullify that. Continue until nothing remains.

If you are truly worthy of such nullification, then your soul will be included in its Root, which is God, the Necessary Existence. All the world will then be included in this Root along with your soul.

Hitbodedut-meditation is the best and the highest level of worship. Set aside an hour or more each day to meditate, in the fields or in a room, pouring out your thoughts to God. Make use of arguments and persuasion, with words of grace, longing and petition, supplicating God and asking that He bring you to serve Him in truth.

Such meditation should be in the language that you normally speak. It is difficult to express your thoughts in Hebrew, and the heart is therefore not drawn after the words. We do not normally speak Hebrew, and are not accustomed to expressing yourself in this language. It is therefore much easier to express yourself in your native language.

In your everyday native language, express all your thoughts to God, speaking of everything that is in your heart. This can involve regret and repentance for the past, or requests and supplications asking that you should truly come close to God in the future. Every person can express his own thoughts, each according to his level.

You should be very careful with this practice, accustoming yourself to do it at a set time each day. The rest of the day can then be joyous.

This is a very great practice. It is the best possible advice, including all things. It is good for everything that may be lacking in your relationship with God. Even if you are completely removed from God, you should still express your thoughts to Him, and ask [that He bring you back].

Even if your words are blocked, and you cannot open your mouth to God, you can still prepare yourself to do so. Even getting ready to speak to God is in itself very good. Even though you cannot speak to Him, you long and yearn to do so - and this itself is very good.

You can even make a prayer out of this itself. You can cry out to God that you are so far from Him that you cannot even speak. You can ask Him to have mercy on you and open your mouth so that you should be able to express your thoughts to Him.

You should know that many great, famous saints (*Tzaddikim*) said that they only reached their high level through this practice of *Hitbodedut*-meditation. If you have wisdom, you will understand the importance of this practice, and how it brings one higher and higher.

Yet, it is something that can be done equally by every individual, great and small alike. Everyone can observe this practice and reach the highest levels. Happy is he who does so.

You should be consistent in your meditation, expressing your thoughts before God each day.

Even if you cannot speak at all, you should simply repeat a single word, and this, too, is very good. If you can say nothing else, remain firm, and repeat this word over and over again, countless times. You can spend many days with this one word alone, and this will be very beneficial. Remain firm, repeating your word or phrase countless times. God will eventually have mercy on you and open your heart so that you will be able to express all your thoughts.

Speech has great power. It is even possible to prevent a gun from firing. Understand this.

You must be worthy to be able to meditate for a given time each day, [thinking about your life] and regretting what you must. Not everyone can have such mental tranquility each day. The days pass and are gone, and you find that you never once had time to really think.

You must therefore make sure to set aside a specific time each day to calmly review your life. Consider what you are doing, and ponder whether it is worthwhile for you to devote your life to it.

A person who does not meditate cannot have wisdom. He may occasionally be able to concentrate, but not for any length of time. His power of concentration remains weak and cannot be maintained.

If a person does not meditate, he also does not realize the foolishness of the world. But when an individual has a relaxed and penetrating mind, he can see that it is all meaningless.

It is best to meditate in the meadows outside the city. Go to a grassy field, and the grass will awaken your heart.

Know that when you pray in the fields, all the grasses come into your prayers. They help you and give you strength to pray.

It is for this reason that prayer is called *Sichah*. This shares a root with the word for grass, as in, "All the grass *(Si 'ach)* of the field..." (*Genesis 2:5*).

It is thus written, "And Isaac went out to meditate *(Suach)* in the field" (Genesis 24:63). His prayer was helped and strengthened by the field, since all the grasses fortified and aided his prayer.

Rabbi Nachman said that the main time that King David would meditate upon God was at night, under the covers in bed. Hidden from the sight of all others, he would pour out his heart before God. He therefore said, "I meditate every night on my bed in tears" (*Psalms 6:7*).

It is very good to have a special room, set aside for Torah study and prayer. Such a room is especially beneficial for secluded meditation and conversation with God.

Rabbi Nachman said that it is very good even to sit in such a special room. The atmosphere itself is beneficial, even if you sit there and do nothing.

Even if you do not have a special room, you can still meditate and express your thoughts to God.

Rabbi Nachman said that you can create your own "special room" under your Tallit. Just drape your Tallit over your eyes and express your thoughts to God as you desire.

You can also meditate with God in bed under the covers. This was King David's custom, as he said, "I meditate every night on my bed in tears" (*Psalms 6:7*).

You can also converse with God while sitting before an open book. Let others think that you are merely [reading or] studying.

There are many other ways in which you can accomplish this if you truly want to meditate and express your thoughts to God. Above all else, this is the root and foundation of holiness and repentance.

Elijah was an ordinary human being, living in this world. But through secluded meditation, he reached such a high level that he never tasted death.

From Rabbi Nachman's words, it was obvious that Elijah reached his high level only through this practice. The same is true of all the other great saints.

***

We have already seen that meditation was very important in the career of the prophets. Since this fact is not very well recognized, however, it would be useful to look at a number of classical sources that speak of this explicitly. As we shall see, a good number of the most influential classical Judaic philosophers and Kabbalists clearly stated that meditation was the most important of all disciplines required to attain enlightenment and prophecy.

There are sources dating from Talmudic times which teach that prophecy involves a very high degree of mental quietude. Jeremiah's disciple, Baruch ben Neriah said, "I have not found serenity," and a very ancient Midrash comments, "Serenity is nothing other than prophecy." The spiritual power and enlightenment that is the most important element of the prophetic experience is not found in the whirlwind or earthquake, but in the "still small voice" of utter tranquillity. This is a state that is attained through deep meditation.

Rabbi Isaac Abarbanel (1437-1508), one of the most influential Bible commentators and philosophers speaks of meditation in the context of prophecy in a number of places. He states that the first step in prophecy is to attain a strong level of desire to bind oneself to God, and this must then be followed by intense meditation.

Elsewhere he teaches that the prophets used to have a special place for their meditations. After Saul attempted to strike David with a spear, the scripture states that "David fled and escaped and he came to Samuel in Ramah.... He and Samuel then went to Naiot, where they remained" *(I Samuel 19:18)*, Abarbanel writes, "It appears that Naiot was a place near Ramah, where the prophets stayed. It was a place set aside for their meditations *(hitbodedut)*, where they would go and seek the word of God. The Targum therefore states that it was the "Academy of the Prophets."

The prophets would meditate *(hitboded)* on the highest mysteries of the Sefirot, as well as on the Supernal Soul, which includes all attributes.

They would depict these things in their mind with their imaginative faculty, visualizing them as if they were actually in front of them.

When their soul became attached to the Supernal Soul, this vision would be increased and intensified. It would then be revealed automatically through a state where thought is utterly absent.

It was in this manner that the early saints would raise their thoughts, reaching the place from which their souls emanated.

This was also the method of attaining prophecy. The prophet would meditate *(hitboded)*, directing his heart and attaching his mind on high.

What the prophet would visualize would depend on the degree and means of his attachment. He would then gaze and know what would happen in the future.

This is the meaning of the verse, "To Him shall you cleave" *(Deuteronomy 10:20).*

> *Rabbi Menachem Recanati (1123-1290),*
> *Master Kabbalist.*

***

Prophecy is a spiritual influx granted by God to man. It is obvious that the individual must prepare himself for such perfection, by binding himself to God and constant meditation *(hitbodedut)* in His worship.

It is also obvious that this attachment and bond to God is attained through the Torah and its commandments, which contain the ultimate perfection of man.

The proper way of attaining this level is through true love and worship of God. It is obvious that if one strengthens this bond of love, he will be all the more ready for enlightenment. When an individual maintains this bond consistently and meditates *(hitboded)* deeply in his love of God, there is no question that the divine influx will be granted him, providing that there is nothing to prevent it.

> *Rabbi Chasdai Cresces (1340-1410)*
> *Philosopher.*

***

With his keen mind, [Moses] was able to understand what was required to attain enlightenment, realizing that the path was through meditation *(hitbodedut).*

He therefore chose to separate himself from all who would disturb him and to reject all physical desires, choosing to be a shepherd in the desert, where no people are to be found. While he was there he unquestionably attained a great attachment to the conceptual, divesting himself of all bodily desires, until he was able to remain for forty days and nights without eating or drinking.

Rabbi Simon ben Tzemach Duran (1361-1444),
Philosopher and Commentator.

***

It is written [that Samuel told Saul], "...When you come to the city, you shall meet a band of prophets, coming from the high place, with harp, drum, flute and lyre, and they will be prophesying themselves *(mit-navim)*. The spirit of God shall then succeed in you and you shall prophesy yourself with them, and you shall be transformed into a different man" *(I Samuel 10:5-6)*.

These individuals were the "sons of the prophets," the disciples of Samuel. He taught and directed them, preparing them to perceive the prophetic influx. They would go to this hill to meditate *(hitboded)* and seek prophecy because of the influence of the Ark of God, which was kept there.

While seeking prophecy, they made use of musical instruments, preparing themselves through the elation produced by the music.

When the scripture says that they were "prophesying themselves" *(mit-navim)*, it does not mean that they were singing praise, as stated by a number of commentaries. Rather it means they were inducing prophecy in themselves through meditation *(hitbodedut)*. The word *Mit-nave* is the reflexive form of the word *Nava*, meaning "to prophesy."

The verse then says, "The spirit of God shall succeed in you." In my opinion, this means the *Ruach HaKodesh* would "succeed" in him, this referring to the will and desire for prophecy. The scripture then says that he would attain his desired goal: "You will be transformed into a man." He would attain the prophetic influx, and through this, he would become a different person.

This indicates that the first step in prophecy is a strong desire. This is followed by meditation *(hitbodedut),* which is its means. The goal is then the influx that comes to him.

Rabbi Isaac Abarbanel

***

The concept of a prophetic dream and that of a vision are so close to each other that they can be considered the same. The reason for this is that they both have the same source….

Such a prophetic dream comes through meditation *(hitbodedut)* involving the mind and consciousness. As a result of the power of this meditation on a subject in the mind, a strong impression is made on the soul. Through this meditation, the soul elevates itself, just as if it were separated from the body, and it is not restrained by the body.

This is actually the meaning of the word *Chalom* meaning "dream." It comes from the root *Chalam,* meaning "to strengthen," as in "You strengthened me *(tachlime-ni)* and gave me life" *(Isaiah 38:16).* The reason for this is because a dream is caused by the strength *(chalam)* and vitality of the soul, when it overcomes the body. When one is in a state of preparation through meditation *(hitbodedut),* he is strengthened through a prophetic dream.

A prophetic vision is also the result of meditation. The prophet mentally gazes at the glorious visions involving the mystery of the Chambers on high, binding them together and unifying them on high with their Cause. His mind soars among the fearsome Forms which are in each chamber, and his consciousness is bound to them and unified with them.

Through this, the prophet divests himself of the physical, abandoning all feeling and sensation associated with the body. He dissolves himself in those Forms, and his consciousness becomes clothed in them. Through these forms he experiences his vision, seeing according to the level of his perception.

It is in this manner that one receives a prophetic message, and the words are engraved *(chakak)* in his heart in a spiritual manner.

After the vision leaves him, he divests himself of the Form in which he was garbed through the power of his original form. This is alluded to in the Torah, which says:

"God left when He finished speaking to Abraham, and Abraham returned to his place" *(Genesis 18:33)*. Abraham returned to his original level, where he was before he had this vision.

I have a seen a similar concept in the teachings of the Masters of Truth, who received it from the Gaonim. They write:

"All the faculties of the prophets and seer faint, and they are transmitted from Form to Form, until the individual is clothed in the power of the Form that is revealed to him. This power is then transmuted in the prophet, it gives him the power to receive the prophetic potential.

This is then engraved in his heart with a spiritual form that he depicts. After this agent overwhelms him, thus performing its function, the prophet then divests himself of the power of the Form revealed to him, and he garbs himself in the power of his normal form. It is as if he divests himself of one form and invests himself in another.

The parts of the prophet's mind are then reunited and his original faculties once again return, as they were originally. Then when he is in a normal human state, he speaks the words of his prophecy."

These are the words that I found.

Rabbi Meir ibn Gabbai (1480-1547),
Kabbalistic Philosopher.

***

One must learn these methods from a master, just as the "sons of the prophets," who would prepare themselves for prophecy.

They would also have to put themselves in a joyous mood. This is the significance of Elisha's remark, "'Now bring me a musician.' And it was when the musician played, [and the hand of God came upon him]" *(2 Kings 3:15).*

They would then meditate *(hitboded)* according to their knowledge of the meditative methods. Through this, they would attain wondrous levels, divesting themselves of the physical, and making the mind overcome the body completely. The mind becomes so overpowering that the physical senses are abandoned, and the prophet does not sense anything with them at all.

The prophet's consciousness is then on that which he is seeking, climbing the various orders of steps on high. It was in this manner that they would meditate and divert themselves from the physical.

Rabbi Moses Cordovero (1520-1577).

***

During the time of the prophets, there was no real formal worship service, and each person would pray in his own words. If a special prayer was needed to channel a particular level of spiritual energy, such a service could be led by one of the prophets or their disciples, who knew how to word the prayer to channel the required forces. It is for this reason that a prayer leader is called a *Chazan*, from the same root as *Chazon*, meaning a prophetic vision.

When prophecy ceased, however, this was no longer possible. A formal system of worship, including all its mystical elements, had to be formulated. This was done by the Great Assembly, under the leadership of Ezra, shortly after the return from the Babylonian Exile. It is significant that a number of the last prophets took part in compiling these prayers.

Many of the prophetic traditions were transmitted to the sages of the Talmud and beyond, An excellent account of this is provided by Rabbi Chaim Vital in his introduction to the *Gates of Holiness (Shaarey Kedushah)*.

An Excerpt from
THE GATES OF HOLINESS

"I have seen men of elevation and they are few." [1] Certain individuals yearn to ascend, but the ladder is hidden from their eyes. They contemplate the earlier books, seeking to find the path of life, the way they must go and the deeds they must do in order to elevate their souls to the highest Root, to bind themselves to God. This alone is the eternal

This was the way of the prophets. All their days they would bind themselves to their Creator. As a result of this attachment, *Ruach HaKodesh* would descend on them, teaching them the path leading to the Light. This would then open their eyes to the mysteries of the Torah, this being the subject of King David's prayer. "Open my eyes, and let me gaze at the wonders of your Torah" *(Psalms 119:18)*. They would be led along a straight path, prepared by the "men of elevation," so that they should reach their goal.

After the prophets, came the Early Saints *(Chasidim Rishonim)*, who were also called the Pharisees *(Secluded Ones)*. [2] They sought to follow the ways of the prophets and to imitate their methods.

These individuals would travel to rocky caves and deserts, secluded from the affairs of society. Some would seclude themselves in their homes, as isolated as those who went into the deserts.

---

[1] Paraphrasing Succah 45b. [2] The "Early Saints" (Chasidim Rishonim) are mentioned a number of times in the Talmud, as are the Pharisees (Perushim). Although the Pharisees are frequently maligned, they were among the greatest saints and mystics of their age.

Day and night, they would continuously praise their Creator, repeating the words of Torah, and chanting the Psalms, which gladden the heart. They would continue in this manner until their minds were strongly bound to the Supernal Lights with powerful yearnings. All their days they would do this consistently until they reached the level of *Ruach HaKodesh*, "prophesying and not stopping." [3]

Even though these individuals were on a much lower level than the prophets, we are still ignorant of their ways and methods. We do not know how these holy men served God so that we should be able to emulate them.

In the generations following these individuals, people's hearts became smaller and understanding reduced. Masters of *Ruach HaKodesh* went to their final rest and ceased to exist among us. They left us bereft, hungering and thirsting, until hopelessness grew in the hearts of men and they ceased to seek out this wondrous discipline. All that were left were "two or three berries on the uppermost branch," [4] "one in a city, and two in a family." [5] "They seek water and there is none," [6] "for every vision has been sealed off." [7] All this is because there was no book teaching the method of how to come close and approach the innermost sanctuary.

Some bound angels with oaths making use of Divine Names. They sought light, but found darkness. The angels with which they communicated were very lowly angels, overseers of the physical world, who combined good and evil. These angels themselves could not perceive the Truth and the Highest Lights. They therefore revealed mixed concepts, consisting of good and evil, truth and falsehood, as well as useless ideas involving medicine, alchemy, and the use of amulets and incantations. [8]

These too "erred with strong drink." [9] What they should have done was

---

[3] Paraphrasing Numbers 11:25. [4] Paraphrasing Isaiah 17:6.
[5] Paraphrasing Jeremiah 3:14. [6] Paraphrasing Isaiah 41:17. [7] Paraphrasing Daniel 9:24.
[8] See Sefer Chasidim 205, 206. [9] Paraphrasing Isaiah 28:7.

spend their time studying the Torah and its commandments.

They should have learned a lesson from the four spiritual giants who entered into the Mysteries *(Pardes),* where none escaped whole other than the pious elder Rabbi Akiva. The angels even wanted to strike him down, but God helped him, and "he entered in peace and left in peace" *(Chagigah 14b, 15b).*

These individuals sought very high levels, close to actual prophecy, and it was for that reason that they were injured. But even we today, can be worthy of the lower levels of *Ruach HaKodesh.* This can be through the revelation of Elijah, to which many were worthy, as is well known. It can also consist of revelation of the souls of saints *(Tzaddikim),* which is mentioned several times in the *Zohar.* Even in our own times, I have seen holy men attaining this.

There are also cases where a person's own soul becomes highly purified and is revealed to him, leading him in all his ways. All these are ways of approaching [God], and they can be attained even today by those who are worthy. But this requires much discipline and many temptations before one arrives at the Truth. If one is not sufficiently prepared, another, unclean spirit may enter him....

I am therefore writing a book in which I will explain these mysteries ... as I learned them from the lips of the saintly Rabbi Isaac Luria. Since these involve the deepest secrets and most hidden mysteries, for every handbreadth that I reveal, I will hide a mile. With great difficulty, I will open the gates of holiness, making an opening like the eye of a needle, and let him who is worthy pass through it to enter the innermost chamber. God is good and He will not withhold this benefit from those who walk in righteousness.

THE ESSENCE OF A PERSON

An excerpt from *Tsohar* (Light) - A translation and commentary on one of Rebbe Nachman's lessons by Avraham Greenbaum

At Rebbe Nachman's request Rabbi Nathan used the ideas in *Likutey Moharan* and Rebbe Nachman's other teachings to throw light on the meaning of the laws in the *Shulchan Aruch*, the standard legal compendium covering all aspects of the life of the Jew. The eight volumes of *Likutey Halachot* follow the order of the headings of the laws in the *Shulchan Aruch*, with a number of discourses on each subject. In the course of these often wide-ranging discourses, Rabbi Nathan discusses ideas and passages from throughout TaNaCh, the Talmud and Midrashim, etc. as well as throwing much light on the meaning and application of Rebbe Nachman's teachings. The following two extracts from *Likutey Halachot* both relate to the theme of Tsohar.

Go to Yourself

> God said to Abraham: "*Lech-lecha*: Go to yourself! Go from your country,
> your family and your father's house to the land that I will show you…"
> (Genesis 12:1)

Abraham was the first to show the world the truth. That is why he achieved everything explained in the Rebbe's lesson of Tsohar and the related lesson of "The deeps, they cover them." Thus Abraham was given the Land of Israel, and he attained true prayer and the power to rise above nature. "Go from your country…to the land that I will show you." This was the Land of Israel, which Abraham inherited. "And I will make you a great nation." (Genesis 12:2). The Rabbis taught us that this was a hint to Abraham that his descendants, the Jewish People, would say "the God of Abraham" in all their prayers. Abraham's unwavering truthfulness, his honesty and purity brought him to perfect prayer – so much so that we mention his name in all our prayers.

Yet the opening words of the Hebrew narrative are unusual: *lech lecha* literally means "go to yourself." God was telling Abraham to work to bring himself to the holiness of Eretz Yisrael, and to master the ways of prayer and faith so as to rise beyond nature. The only way is through truth. God said "Go *to yourself*," because the whole journey must be into yourself. It must be a journey to the inner point of truth which is the very source of your being and your life.

The real essence of a person is his soul or spiritual self: "I". When we speak about our body we speak about the body as belonging *to* us: "My body," "your body," etc. This is because the body is subordinate, it is not the whole person. The real essence of a person is the divine soul. This is part of God above - and God is the essence of Truth. That is why the Jewish People, all descendants of Abraham are spoken of as being "all the offspring of *truth*" (Jeremiah 2:21).

So *lech lecha* means: Go *into* yourself. Go to the essential point of truth within you, *your* truth. This alone is called "I" when one speaks about oneself, and only this is called "you" when talking to somebody else in direct speech. Your whole journey, physical as well as spiritual should be into yourself – the essential point of truth rooted within you. Pay no attention to the voices of falsehood, tempting and alluring as they may be. The world is darkened by falsehood, and it is hard to stand up to. But you must take yourself in hand and relentlessly search out the truth. Don't let yourself be fooled.

There were three things God told Abraham to leave behind: "Your country, your family and your father's home." One's native country, his town or city and the society and culture he comes from, breed all kinds of false notions. If you want to eat a piece of fruit, before you get to the fruit itself you have to remove the peal, the *kelipah*. Similarly, in every country, even though there may be a lot of good, there are also all kinds of other factors obscuring the truth and creating darkness. In most societies the majority of people are primarily interested in material concerns, status and other worldly desires. They behave as if this is the path decreed from Mount Sinai. To grow spiritually you have to get away from all this. "Go from your country": leave such things behind and go into yourself, to the point of truth which is the real you. For if you think carefully about the truth, you will see very clearly that pursuits like these will not bring you to the ultimate good of the World to Come.

"Go…from your family." One also has to rid himself of the darkness clinging to him because of the way that he was conceived – for "I was brought forth from iniquity, and in sin did my mother conceive me" (Psalms 51:7).

"And go from your father's home": There are all kinds of foolishness and falsehood that cling to a person because of his home background. For example, some families take excessive pride in their family lineage. They seem to think they deserve special esteem. There are many other kinds of similar foolishness.

God told Abraham to distance himself from all these things and go to the essential point of truth. This alone is the whole man. Then will you come to "the land which I will show you" – the Land of Israel – and "I will make you a great nation": you will attain prayer and truth and have the power to transcend nature.

It is impossible to explain all this in print. If you genuinely want the truth, however, you will understand. Rebbe Nachman said that other people can be the biggest obstacle in life – more so than the evil urge itself. In some cases this is obvious. It is not hard to recognize open scoffers, cynics and trouble-makers. Far more insidious are the people who are genuinely God-fearing yet they offer confusing advice and guidance that is not really suited to one's actual situation. This problem may appear in many different guises.

There is only one answer: always work towards the essential point of truth within. *Lech lecha:* "Go to yourself," It takes much prayer and meditation. We must always try to speak truthfully. But if we do, we will always be moving forward to the truth!

(*Likutey Halachot, Choshen Mishpat, Hilchot Genevah* 5:5, 7-8)

The Truth doesn't have to be harsh

Truth should draw us closer to God, not push us further away. We have to sift out the point of truth which exists in every single Jew, even those who are very far from God. For there is a truth at every level of creation, even in the places and situations that seem furthest away from God. Revealing this truth is the real will of God.

The Torah ends with the words, "the great and awesome deeds which Moses wrought in the eyes of all Israel" (Deuteronomy 34:12). The Rabbis taught that this is an allusion to how Moses broke the two tablets of stone in the eyes of all the Israelites. Each year on Simchat Torah when we conclude the reading of the entire Torah, we immediately go back to the beginning of the Torah: Bereshit, "In the beginning God created..." (Genesis 1:1). It is written "The beginning of your word is truth" (Psalms 119:160) – and the Rabbis pointed out that the last letters of the first three words in the Torah, בראשית ברא אלהים – BereshiT barA ElokiM, spell out the word אמת – EMeT, truth.

In essence the whole creation came about through truth. It is truth that sustains the whole universe. On the other hand, the Midrash tells us that when God said, "Let us make man" (Genesis 1:26), Truth stepped forward to oppose the creation on the grounds that the world would be full of lies. God then took the truth and cast it to the ground, as it is written, "And You have cast truth down to the ground" (Daniel 8:12). Afterwards God said, Let the truth rise up from the earth, as it is written "Truth springs forth from the ground" (Psalms 85:12; Bereshit Rabbah 5:8).

This Midrash makes it seem as if Truth did not agree to the creation. Yet we know that the innermost essence of truth is God Himself, and since, as we see, God created the world, it must be that the whole world was created in accordance with absolute truth. To explain the contradiction, we must understand that God's own truth is awesomely profound and exalted – for His "thoughts are very deep" (Psalms 92:6). So deep, indeed, that even Truth itself as it were – i.e. the angels who express the quality of truth – were unable to comprehend just how far God's intentions reached. This is why they began to stand in accusation, as related in the Midrash. They opposed the creation on the grounds that the world would be full of falsehood. But God has no desire for a truth which seeks to reject the creation entirely – the kind of truth which makes people oppose their friends and reject them because they believe according to their own criteria of truth their friends have strayed from the path. There are times when a person rejects even himself, pushing himself further away from God because of a certain truth inside him – a truth which tells him that he is full of blemishes. This "truth" only pushes him into despair. Such attitudes are rooted in Truth's accusation against the creation as related in the Midrash.

Yet God Himself has no delight in this variety of truth. He casts it away, throwing it down to the earth. The truth God cherishes is that which draws people nearer to Him, not a truth that alienates them. The world may very well be full of falsehood, but in just such a world, when a person stirs himself, searches for and finally attains the point of truth, this is all the more precious to God than anything. This was the purpose of the entire creation, founded as it is on Truth – that inner essence of truth which goes even beyond the comprehension of the angels.

When the Children of Israel sinned with the Golden Calf they ought to have been condemned to complete destruction according to the strict, true law of the Torah. Moses knew this. But he also knew on a higher level of truth God did not want this. That is why Moses cast the tablets – the truth – to the ground and turned to prayer. He knew and believed that God's own truth and wisdom go far beyond man's ability to comprehend. For His thoughts are very deep and His tender lovingkindnesses very many. God does not want to destroy the world. He wants to keep it going. Israel is the very crown of creation. Moses therefore turned to prayer – and succeeded. God was reconciled to him and forgave the Jewish People, commanding Moses to hew out the second tablets. "Let the truth rise up from the earth" – "Truth springs forth from the ground."

This is why, after concluding the Torah with the words "…in the eyes of all Israel", with their allusion to the breaking of the tablets, we immediately begin again with the words "In the beginning," hinting as they do at *God's* Truth, the very essence of truth. This goes far beyond man's ability to comprehend. In the last analysis we ourselves know nothing. We should certainly not allow ourselves to be pushed even further from God because of some notion of truth that we ourselves entertain. With faith in God's truth and lovingkindness we must start again each time and draw ourselves closer to God from the actual situation we find ourselves in. For His lovingkindness is exalted indeed. Every day of our lives we can start again this way, and this is how we draw closer and closer to God.

(*Likutey Halachot, Yoreh De'ah, Hilchot Ribit* 5)

Seeing the Goodness in Life
and making life better for others

One of the secrets to being happy…… is being thankful!

A negative mind will NEVER give you a positive life.

A beautiful heart can bring things into your life
that all the money in the world couldn't obtain.

Friendship is born at the moment when one person says to another,
"What! You too? I thought I was the only one."

Friends are medicine for a wounded heart,
and vitamins for a hopeful soul.

Remember, when you forgive, you heal,
and when you let go, you grow.

Forgiving is a form of giving – to ourselves most of all!

Be kind to others. Your unassuming kindness might become someone's
memory of a lifetime."

Good friends are like stars. You don't always see them,
but you know they are there.

Forgive others, not because they necessarily deserve forgiveness,
but because you deserve peace.

Jumping to conclusions is an unhealthy exercise.

Let the stress go and let blessings flow. Keep your head up and keep
pushing forward. God has a plan. Have faith.

Enjoy the little things in life, for one day you may look back and realize
they were the big things.

The only wealth which you will keep forever
is the wealth you give away.

The heart has no wrinkles and a soul never grows old.

"Anyone can count the seeds in an apple;
only God can count the apples in a seed."

Reb Avigdor Miller

Love and kindness are never wasted. They always make a difference.

Every child is a source of immense joy and light.

Use your smile to change the world,
but don't let the world change your smile.

Make dinner time for your family a gossip-free zone.

A pessimist is one who makes difficulties of his opportunities,
and an optimist is one who makes opportunities of his difficulties.

The positive thinker sees the invisible, feels the intangible,
and achieves the impossible.

Keep looking up…
That's the secret of life…

I was searching for the state of happiness
and realised it's all in the state of mind.

I am currently self-employed, so if you see me talking to myself,
I am just in a staff meeting.

Your extra words hold in. Your extra money hand out.

Making a positive impact in the lives of others
is what makes your own life important.

Life doesn't have to be perfect to be filled with joy.

The healthiest response to life is joy.

The best kind of existence is to exist for others.

You all laugh at me because I am different...
I laugh at you because you are all the same.

The richest person is not the one who has the most,
but the one who needs the least.

We can't help everyone, but everyone can help someone.

Look back and thank God. Look forward and trust God.

You cannot do all the good that the world needs.
But the world needs all the good you can do.

If we were meant to stay in one place, we'd have roots instead of feet.

Happiness is an explosive. It breaks down barriers.

The secret to happiness is being content.

The best way to calm the anxious mind
is to forgive yourselves and others.

"There can be no definition of a successful life that doesn't include
service to others... I have found happiness. I no longer pursue it,
for it is mine."

George W. Bush.

Beauty begins the moment you decide to be yourself.

Beauty is not in the face, beauty is a light in the heart.

"Don't just count your days, make your days count."

Colin Powell.

Hardships often prepare ordinary people for an extraordinary destiny.

People understand your words. Friends understand your silences.

Help from a stranger is better than sympathy from a relative.

Why wish upon a star when you can pray to the one who created it.

The most important decision you will ever make is to be in a good mood.

Be realistic. Trust in the One above.

Love is better than anger. Hope is better than fear. Optimism is better than despair. So let us be loving, hopeful and optimistic. And we will change the world.

He who has a *why* to live can bear to live with any *how*.

Everything will be good in the end…if it's not good it's not the end.

"Your unique contribution to the world is a very specific activity which you love to excel at."

Rabbi Dov Heller.

Life is like riding a bicycle: to keep your balance you need to keep moving forward.

They say a person needs just three things in this world – someone to love, something to do, and something to hope for.

Don't tell God how big your problems are; tell your problems how big God is!

Decide every morning that you are in a good mood.

Never give up. Great things take time.

If you stay positive in a negative situation, you win.

There's no reason to look back when God gives you so much to look forward to.

Life is the biggest bargain. We get it for nothing.

That dream was planted in your heart for a reason.

You can accomplish by kindness what you could not by force.

"We don't make a living… we take a living from God."

Rabbi Mordechai Gifter.

Kindness is the mark we leave on the world.

Start the day off on the right note with a smile and a great attitude.

When life gives you a hundred reasons to cry,
show life you have a thousand reasons to smile.

When you focus on the good, the good gets better.

Our days are happier when we give people a bit of our heart
rather than a piece of our mind.

A beautiful heart will bring things into your life
that all the money in the world couldn't get you.

If we magnified blessings as much as we magnify disappointments,
we would all be much happier.

When I was 5 years old my mother told me that HAPPINESS was the
key to life. When I went to school they asked me what I wanted to be
when I grew up. I wrote down "happy". They told me I didn't
understand the assignment, and I told them they didn't understand life.

Those who are lifting the world upward and onward are those who
encourage more than criticize.

When you pray for others, God listens to you and blesses them and you.
When you are safe and happy, remember that perhaps someone has
prayed for you.

I choose for blissful miracles to become part of my daily reality.

Reflect upon your present blessings – not on your past misfortunes, of which all people have some.

The path to peace of mind is paved with
forgiving more and judging less.

The meaning of life is to find your gift,
the purpose of life is to give it away.

Courage does not always roar. Sometimes courage is the quiet voice at the end of the day that says I will try again tomorrow.

Of course I struggle. I just don't quit.

The best way to understand people is to listen to them.

No he is not perfect, but he is perfect for me, and that's all that matters.

I may not have gone to where I intended to go,
but I think I have ended up where I needed to be.

The first duty of love is to listen.

The most basic of all human needs is
the need to understand and be understood.

HOPE – Help Out People Everywhere.

Respect is love in action.

Knowing that you inspire others can sometimes be your
greatest inspiration.

Don't look back. You are not going that way.

Don't waste words on people who deserve your silence.

Faith is not knowing what the future holds,
but knowing Who holds the future.

There is nothing noble in feeling superior to your fellow man –
true nobility is being superior to your former self.

Unity does not mean sameness – it means oneness of purpose.

Negative people need drama like oxygen.
Stay positive – it will take their breath away.

Good character is the single most important attribute
of a successful and worthy life.

Anger is only one letter short of danger.

What soap is to the body, laughter is to the soul.

People who say it cannot be done
should not interrupt those who are doing it.

Be patient with others as God is patient with us.

The more we give, the more we live.

Worry doesn't help the future, but it sure does ruin the present.

Thank God more and you will find more to thank Him for.

Life is fragile – handle with prayer.

The greatest happiness in the world is to make others happy.

God gave us a fingerprint that no one else has,
so that we can leave an imprint that no one else can.

It's always good to take a break, think and take things easy.

When life knocks you down, roll over and look at the stars.

Health and cheerfulness go hand in hand with each other.

There is nothing more beautiful than someone who
goes out of their way to make life beautiful for others.

If you want God to focus on the good in you,
always seek out the good in others.

If you are not making someone else's life better,
then you are wasting your time.

It's good to be blessed. It's better to be a blessing.

The best speed on the road is… 60 smiles an hour.

God is always near, there is no need to fear.

The best thing we can give others is our time.

The more we accept and the less we expect the happier we will be.

Friendship is a rare type of currency – it never depreciates,
it only appreciates.

Leadership is about empathy. It is about having the ability to relate to
and connect with people for the purpose of inspiring and empowering
their lives.

When we take care of ourselves, we're a better person for others.
When we feel good about ourselves, we treat each other better.

Never let the things you desire make you
forget about the things you have.

The difference between ordinary and extraordinary
is just that little "extra".

Treasure your friends, as true friends are treasures.

A smile is a curve that sets everything straight.

What sunshine is to flowers, smiles are to humanity.

Empathy is simply listening, holding space, withholding judgment, emotionally connecting and communicating that incredibly healing message of "you are not alone".

Only a life lived for others, is worth living.

Some people are so poor that all they have is money.

The more you praise God, the more He will give you reasons to praise Him.

The smallest good deed is better than the grandest intention.

Prayer does not change God, but it does change the one who prays.

To strengthen the muscles of your heart, the best exercise is… lifting someone else's spirit.

The world little notes nor long remembers little acts of kindness… but people do.

If I do what's right, God will do what's left.

The only thing that will make you happy is being happy with who you are, and not what people think you are.

Make living your life with absolute integrity and kindness your first priority.

Even if you don't feel happy, act happy, and then you'll begin to actually feel happy.

Happiness is a way of traveling, not the destination.

The biggest communication is not listening to understand, but listening to reply.

Where hope grows, miracles blossom.

Today is your opportunity to build the tomorrow you want.

Don't call it a dream. Call it a plan.

You have to choose happiness – it doesn't choose you.

When you have an opportunity to help someone in need, do it and do it with joy, because that is God answering that person's prayer.

We make a living by what we get. But we make a life by what we give.

The future belongs to those who believe in the beauty of their dreams.

A spark of encouragement can rekindle warmth in the heart.

The biggest room in the world is the room for improvement.

Don't ruin a good today by thinking about a bad yesterday.

I wish you all the best because you are the best.

Laughter is the shortest distance between two people.

Love is the pleasure of focusing on the virtues of another.

People who shine from within do not need a spotlight on them.

When you can't find the sunshine…be the sunshine.

If you have good thoughts, they will shine out of your face,
and you will always look lovely.

At the height of laughter, the universe is flung into a kaleidoscope of new possibilities.

There is nothing in the world so irresistibly contagious
as laughter and good humor.

Emuna is not about everything turning out ok;
it's about being ok with the way everything turns out.

It isn't where you came from. It's where you're going that counts.

You can't push yourself forward in life by patting yourself on the back.

We can pray for the strength to bring God's light to this world.

The best way to have a happy thought is to count your blessings,
not your cash.

May your troubles be less and your blessings more, and nothing but
happiness come through your door.

The secret of change is to focus all of your energy,
not on fighting the old, but on building the new.

Happiness is not doing what you enjoy, but enjoying what you do.

Happiness is not a goal...it's a by-product of a life well lived.

One of the best feelings in the world is
knowing someone is happy because of you.

Don't confuse your path with your destination.

Just because it's stormy now
doesn't mean you aren't headed for sunshine.

True beauty is born through our actions and aspirations
and in the kindness we offer to others.

The greatest gift you can give someone is your time. Because when you
do you give them a portion of your life that you will never get back.

A person who has good thoughts cannot ever be ugly. If you have good
thoughts they will shine out of your face like sunbeams and you will
always look lovely.

We are valued not by what we get, but by what we contribute.

Health is the greatest possession. Contentment is the greatest treasure.
Confidence is the greatest friend.

Every trial endured and weathered in the right spirit
makes a soul nobler and stronger than it was before.

Sadness shuts the doors of heaven. Prayer opens closed doors,
and joy can shatter fortified walls.

Always find a reason to laugh. It may not add years to your life
but it will surely add life to your years.

Being joyous about God's help is a cure in and of itself.

Learn from yesterday, plan for tomorrow
and live each moment of today.

Consider how hard it is to change yourself, and you will understand
what little chance you have to change another.

The road to success is always under construction.

Example is not the main thing in influencing others, it is the only thing.

Gratitude is a magnet to miracles

Keep your words soft and sweet -- you never know
when you'll have to eat them.

People who have a positive attitude, are inspired, motivated and
passionate about what they believe in, communicate better and
more effectively.

Set your sights high, the higher the better.

Expect the most wonderful things to happen;
not in the future but right now.

There's a lot of difference between listening and hearing.

It is not how much we have,
but how much we enjoy that makes happiness.

Don't wait for the perfect moment.
Take the moment and make it perfect.

The best vitamin for making friends...... B1.

The happiness of your life depends on the quality of your thoughts.

The ability to speak in several languages is an asset.
But the ability to keep your mouth closed in any language is priceless.

No one is in control of your happiness but you; therefore, you have the
power to change anything about yourself or your life that you want
to change.

A kind word is like a spring day.

The capacity to care is the thing which gives life its deepest significance.

It takes a smart person to have the last word and not use it.

If you see something good in another,
it is a reflection of the good in yourself.

Surround yourself with positive souls and positive vibes come naturally.
Your environment influences your experience. Make it a positive one.

A positive attitude causes a chain reaction of positive thoughts,
events and outcomes. It is a catalyst and it sparks extraordinary results.

Enthusiasm finds the opportunities, and energy makes the most of them.

Never stop thanking God because God never stops providing.

You don't earn loyalty in a day. You earn loyalty day-by-day.

Patience is not about waiting,
but the ability to keep a good attitude while waiting.

Smile, it is the key that fits the lock of everybody's heart.

A strong home is built with gentle words.

Life is about making an impact, not making an income.

The best gift to give your friend is your heart.

To get the full value of joy you must have someone to divide it with.

Don't let yesterday take up too much of today.

Being great does not excuse one from being good.

It's not happiness that makes us grateful;
it's the gratefulness that makes us happy.

It does not matter how slowly you go
as long as you are heading in the right direction and do not stop.

Never ruin an apology with an excuse.

A mistake that makes you humble is better than
an achievement that makes you arrogant.

Age is mind over matter. If you don't mind, it doesn't matter.

It's not about how big the house is, it's about how happy the home is.

No matter how long you have traveled in the wrong direction,
you can always turn around.

Education is not something you can 'finish'.

Be humble in your confidence yet courageous in your character.

We are here to add what we can to, not get what we can from life.

Pride is concerned with who is right.
Humility is concerned with what is right.

Sometimes, all you need is for someone to say,
"Chin up, it will all be OK."
Be the one to tell the same to someone else.

Let your hopes, not your hurts, shape your future.

The most fortunate are those who have a wonderful capacity to
appreciate again and again, freshly and naively, the basic goods of life,
with awe, pleasure and wonder.

Appreciation...acknowledges the presence of good wherever you shine
the light of your thankful thoughts.

Remember that there is someone out there that is more than happy with
less than what you have.

Don't put the key to your happiness in someone else's pocket.

You aren't really wealthy until you have something money can't buy.

No matter what the circumstances,
we can always find a reason to thank God.

A friend is someone who knows everything about you --
and likes you anyway.

One child, one teacher, one book, one pen can change the world.

To be yourself in a world that is constantly trying to make you
something else is the greatest accomplishment.

I not only use all the brains I have, but all I can borrow.

Happiness is an inside job.

For lasting happiness look beyond yourself.

We are all handicapped in some way--cheer your smallest steps!
True strength is not physical.

Believe in yourself as much as the One who created you believes in you and gave you a mission you can accomplish.

A happy person is happy, not because everything is right in his life. He is happy because his attitude towards everything in his life is right.

Kindness is in our power, even when fondness is not.

Big, sweeping life changes really boil down to small, everyday decisions.

What you focus on expands, and when you focus on the goodness in your life, you create more of it.

Kindness is a language the deaf can hear and the blind can see.

Alone we can do so little; together we can do so much.

Don't wait for people to be friendly; show them how.

A strong, positive mental attitude will create more miracles than any wonder drug.

Some people think that being positive is not being realistic. Being positive, however, is the true realism.

No one has ever become poor by giving.

Just because it hasn't happened yet, doesn't mean it never will.

By changing the inner attitudes of our minds, we can change the outer aspects of our lives.

We have two ears and one mouth, so we can listen twice as much as we speak.

By swallowing evil words unsaid, no one has ever hurt their stomach.

Failure is when one stops trying, not when one doesn't succeed.

Life isn't tied with a bow, but it's still a gift.

The meaning of life …is to live a meaningful life.
Don't stress and don't try to impress.

Some people make the world more special by being in it.
Be confident and humble at the same time.

Make peace with your past so it won't mess up the present.

Remember that nothing ahead of you is bigger or stronger
than the power of God behind you.

Happy moments praise God
Difficult moments seek God
Quiet moments pray to God
Painful moments trust God
Every moment thank God

A little bit of light pushes away a lot of darkness.

There are two ways to live your life. One is as though nothing is a
miracle. The other is as though everything is a miracle.

The most beautiful thing is to see a person smiling and even more
beautiful, is knowing that you are the reason behind it!!!

Keep the faith and drop the fear.

Life is not about how fast you run or how high you climb,
but how well you bounce.

Healing doesn't mean the damage never existed,
it means the damage no longer controls your life.

Your life is your message. Make it a good one.

Most people are like you and me, or the people across the street or around the world from you and me. Just like you and me, their hearts tell them that somewhere, somehow, they can make a positive difference in the world.

It takes each of us to make a difference for all of us.

Your limitation - it's only your imagination.

If they are wrong, educate them. Don't belittle them.

Life is not measured by the number of breaths we take,
but by the moments that take our breath away.

So many of our dreams at first seem impossible, then they seem improbable, and then, when we summon the will, they soon become inevitable.

Don't let your mistakes define you.

If your compassion does not include yourself, it is incomplete.

Let's forget the baggage of the past and make a new beginning.

"I can" is 100 times more important than IQ.

He who minds another person's business
either has no mind or no business.

Prayer is the pulse of life.

Bring Your Soul Back To Life!

> C harity
> P rayer
> R epentance

Do not look back in anger or forward in fear, but around in awareness.

Do not let the behavior of others destroy your inner peace.

Never underestimate the valuable and important difference you make in every life you touch for the impact you make today has a powerful rippling effect on every tomorrow.

Nobody cares for your beauty if your tongue is ugly.

Your talent is God's gift to you. How you use it is your gift to God.

The difference between stumbling blocks and stepping stones is how you use them.

Speak only when you feel that your words are better than your silence.

Be strong. You never know who you are inspiring.

Everyone has a right to their ideas.
But that doesn't mean everyone's ideas are right.

If the world didn't need you, you wouldn't be here.

Your purpose is the essence of who you are.

Success is not final; failure is not fatal.
It is the courage to continue that counts.

Within every person is a unique flower,
bringing his or her special fragrance to the world.

The word "Can't" has two meanings.
1. It's impossible
2. I don't want to do it.

At least 95% of the time it is used it means -
"I don't want to".
Think about it.

Anything is possible when you have
the right kind of people there to support you.

The best way to not feel hopeless is to get up and do something.
Don't wait for good things to happen to you. If you go out and make
some good things happen, you will fill the world with hope, you will
fill yourself with hope.

Behind every great achievement is a dreamer of great dreams.

Don't let others tell you what you can't do. Don't let the limitations of
others limit your vision. If you can remove your self-doubt and believe
in yourself, you can achieve what you never thought possible.

The good you do today may be forgotten tomorrow.
Do good anyway.

If you scream you're heard
If you talk you're understood
If you smile you're loved.

Excellence is not a skill. It is an attitude.

Three things in human life are important. The first is to be kind.
The second is to be kind. And the third is to be kind.

Constant kindness can accomplish much. As the sun makes ice melt,
kindness causes misunderstanding, mistrust, and hostility to evaporate.

Kindness can become its own motive. We are made kind by being kind.

What lies behind you and what lies in front of you,
pales in comparison to what lies inside of you.

If your soul is what drives you, you will never find yourself lost.

If nothing ever changed, there would be no butterflies.
And if miracles aren't real, you wouldn't be here.

Believe in your heart that you're going to do great things today.

If you will utilize what is in your capacity, eventually you will also acquire what lies beyond your capacity.

Laughter is truly one of the "Secrets of Life."
Find people who make you laugh and howl with utter joy!

How beautiful is it to stay silent
when someone expects you to be enraged.

Let us be grateful to the people who make us happy;
they are the charming gardeners who make our souls blossom.

Today only happens once... make it amazing.

Put on a coat and you will be warm.
Build a fire and we will all be warm.

Gratitude can transform common days into thanksgivings, turn routine jobs into joy, and change ordinary opportunities into blessings.

Avoid excuses and you will be successful.

If you focus on what you have in life, you'll always have more.
If you focus on what you don't have in life, you'll never have enough.

In helping others, we shall help ourselves, for whatever good we give out completes the circle and comes back to us.

Happiness is when what you think, what you say,
and what you do are in harmony.

Treating your kids with respect is the best way
to teach them to respect you.

Life isn't about waiting for the storm to end.
It's about learning to dance in the rain.

When you hold grudges your hands aren't free to catch blessings

Good friends are like a box of fancy chocolates.
It's what's inside that makes them special!

Never let words of encouragement go unsaid.

"Stop trying to perfect your child, but keep trying to perfect your
relationship with him."

Dr. Henker.

Let your joy be in your journey—not in some distant goal.

Once you replace negative thoughts with positive ones,
you'll start having positive results.

A smile can transform an obstacle into a bridge.

It's hard to find happiness within ourselves,
but it's impossible to find it anywhere else.

True friends are the ones who walk in
when the rest of the world walks out.

Peace does not mean to be in a place where there is no noise,
trouble or hard work. It means to be in the midst of those things
and still be calm in your heart.

Fear less, hope more; Eat less, chew more; Whine less, breathe more;
Talk less, say more; Love more, and all good things will be yours!

You cannot shake hands with a clenched fist.

Don't look back unless it's a good view.

Nothing is more beautiful than the smile
that has struggled through the tears.

Just when the caterpillar thought that life was over, it became a butterfly.

When someone tells you: "It can't be done!"
Remember: Those are their limits, not yours.

Doing well is the result of doing good.

You need unity, you don't need uniformity.

Be so happy that when others look at you, they become happy too.

I can't change the past but I can choose not to ruin the present
by worrying about the future.

When you stop expecting people to be perfect
you can like them for who they are.

It is health that is real wealth and not pieces of gold and silver.

Everything comes to you at the right time. Be patient.

Greatness is not found in possessions, power, position, or prestige.
It is discovered in goodness, humility, service, and character.

The best antidote to annoyance is an act of love.

Reb Shlomo's Wisdom

some heartwarming words from Shlomo Carlebach

"Now I want you to know the deepest depths. Every person has a share in this world and the world to come. We understand the concept of a share in the world to come, but what does it mean having a share in this world? Open your hearts. Having a share in this world means I know exactly what I have to do in this world. This is a very high level. If I know that if I don't do it, it just won't happen. Then I've just got to do it. This is my share in this world."

"Evil is always new. Imagine, if you do something wrong, you swear to yourself you'll never do it again, right? How come evil returns the next day? The answer is very simple. Evil has a newness. So how do you fight evil? With even more newness."

"Abraham was the first Jew, the first messenger of God on earth. The first thing Abraham did was to open his house, in fact he took away the doors. Everybody was welcome. Abraham didn't preach to the sinners, 'Listen you dirty pagans, you are going to hell.' He just took them in and told them, 'This is my house and this is your house too.' "

"Tears flow up. When you see someone's tears flowing from their eyes, they are not going down.... Gevalt, are they going up to heaven! Gevalt, are they going up! When somebody is crying, God gives you the greatest, deepest privilege... to kiss away their tears!"

"What is it to really have a covenant with God? A lot of people have a covenant with God and they are God drunk. They don't see the people anymore, especially if the people are pagans, according to their theory. A person who has a true covenant with God has to be completely aware of every little pagan in the world. If Abraham would not have welcomed the three angels who were disguised as pagans, we would never have had Isaac and there would never be a Messiah, and the whole world would probably have been destroyed one way or another."

"People walk around sad because they don't know what to do with their future. You have this minute right now. What are you doing with it? The difference between sadness and joy is very simple. Sadness always tells you: 'Oy vey! What are you going to do in ten minutes? What will you do ten years from now?' If you are really filled with joy for one minute, then you will know what to do for the next minute also. What is God giving you? He is giving you this minute. He hasn't given you tomorrow. Of course I don't know what to do tomorrow, because I didn't receive it yet. Sadness is very concerned with what I don't have, and I really don't have tomorrow yet. The truth is, I am always standing before nothingness, because I am non-existent yet for the next minute. I am not here yet. Time isn't there. The world isn't there. The world is here … right now!"

"We have 613 mitzvot (commandments), 613 laws. I don't like the word 'laws' because they are not laws. The word law reminds you of police, some straight character sitting there telling you what to do. Very bad translation. 'Mitzvah' means that God gave us 613 ways to come closer to Him. The ways are divided into two parts, 248 ways of reaching God by doing certain things, and 365 ways of reaching Him by not doing certain things. If there is a red light and I don't go, nothing happens, right? I just don't cross the street. However, if God's red light flashed and I stop when I have a chance to do wrong, then something happens inside me. Something happened to me; I walked a few steps higher."

"I often mention Holy Beggars, but people ask me who really is a Holy Beggar? Open your hearts my beautiful friends. A Holy Beggar is someone who is begging you to allow him to give!"

"If your ears are not open to the crying of the poor, then your ears are deaf, and you will not hear God calling either."

"The more real a thing is the less you can see it. After you reach the level where you see all the things which are not to be seen, then you open your eyes and everything is clear to you, and it feels like you saw it all the time. To love someone is the deepest thing in the world, but you can't prove it. You can't put your finger on it, but it is the most real thing in the world. God is the most, utmost real thing in the world and you can't see Him, but after you don't see Him, you see Him. Then you can see Him everywhere, in the flower, in every cloud, in every little stone, in every candle. When we say the Shema, God is One, we close our eyes, because first we don't see God, we're blind, we just believe, but then we open our eyes and it is so clear, He's always there."

"Everybody likes God to do miracles, but the big question is, are you a miracle? If you are living on the level of miracles, if you trust in God on the level of a miracle, then miracles happen to you. If you are not living your life on that level, then miracles don't happen to you."

"You are born into the world, but until someone comes to you and tells you 'I love you,' you are still a stranger in the world. You feel like a stranger – you're not really here yet. The *Zohar Kadosh* says to take a stranger and invite him into my house means I am giving this person even more existence than God gave him. God sent him into this world and he is here, but this is not real existence. The real existence of a person has to be given by another person. What happens if I drink a Coca Cola and make a *brocha* over it, what am I doing to the Coca Cola? I am giving it existence! Because so far the Coca Cola was like nothing. Or imagine I say hello to a little dog. What am I doing to the dog? I'm giving him existence. He was like a little stranger walking around in the world. And you know what my sweetest friends? Even

God needs us to give Him existence! God is there, but until I really say He's there, He's not really there."

"There is a saying that everything in the world is here for the service of God. Somebody once came to Reb Alexander and asked him how can you serve God by being an atheist? Reb Alexander answered that you have to be an atheist when someone asks a favour of you. If you believe in God, then deep down you'll think, 'I'll pray for you, I'll bless you, but I don't have to do anything, because God will do it.' So when someone asks a favour of you, my most beautiful friends, you have to be a complete atheist because God won't do anything for him, *you* have got to do it!"

"Sometimes someone asks a favor which is very hard. We don't have the faintest idea what a favor the person is doing by asking! At that very moment God is opening gates for us, giving us a chance to have the image of God on our face again. We have to wash and polish ourselves, but sometimes there is so much dirt that soap and water aren't enough, we have to rub and scratch the dirt off. Even that isn't enough sometimes, and we have to go to a sauna. You have to do a mitzvah on the level of a sauna, burning hot. Sweat it out."

"There is a passage in the Psalms, 'Let the sin go away, not the sinners.' If I see someone doing wrong, I am angry, not at the person, but at what he is doing. As the Baal Shem Tov once said, the real person is not involved in the wrong-doing. He is like half asleep. So *gevalt* I am angry! 'Why aren't you awake?' But I can't really be too angry, because he was asleep. The question is, if you are angry, are you getting angry at the person, or at the evil? If you are a *neshama* person, there is no hatred. If you have hatred, then you are evil also."

"All of God's wisdom is encased in a garment: it is in the music. When we speak, you say 'yes' and I say 'no' and we are already opposed to each other. In music, what is absolutely unbelievable, is that I can sing a melody, you can sing different notes, and it's the deepest harmony. The greatest revelation of God's oneness in the world is music."

"If God had given me two hearts, I could use one for hating and the other one for love. But since I was given only one heart, I have only room for love."

Hebrew: The Root of Language

Bereishit - Genesis - Chapter 11

1Now the entire earth was of one language and one speech.

2And it came to pass when they traveled from the east, that they found a valley in the land of Shinar and settled there.

3And they said to one another, "Come, let us make bricks and fire them thoroughly"; so the bricks were to them for stones, and the clay was to them for mortar.

4And they said, "Come, let us build ourselves a city and a tower with its top in the heavens, and let us make ourselves a name, lest we be scattered upon the face of the entire earth."

5And the Lord descended to see the city and the tower that the sons of man had built.

6And the Lord said, "Lo! [they are] one people, and they all have one language, and this is what they have commenced to do. Now, will it not be withheld from them, all that they have planned to do?

7Come, let us descend and confuse their language, so that one will not understand the language of his companion."

8And the Lord scattered them from there upon the face of the entire earth, and they ceased building the city.

9Therefore, He named it Babel, for there the Lord confused the language of the entire earth, and from there the Lord scattered them upon the face of the entire earth.

The great medieval commentator Rashi (Rabbi Shlomo Yitzchaki) informs us that the sages of old knew full well that the original language that all mankind spoke, prior to the confusion of tongues following the Tower of Babel, was Hebrew.

To support this contention, Isaac Mozeson has traced the roots of tens of thousands of words in numerous languages from around the world back to their original Hebrew sources.

Below is a list of a few English examples that he shows from his arduous and extensive study, that gives the English words, and their suggested Hebrew roots with their meanings, often giving their biblical sources:

Abash - Bi'esh; Boosh - To be ashamed

Abbot - (Greek) Abbas - Abba - Father

Aberration - Aveirah - Sin

Accelerate - Kal - Swift

Accoutrements - (French) Couture - Choot - Thread

Acme - Kooma - Height - I Kings 6:2

Acumen - Chochmah - Wisdom

Add - Od - More

A(d)miral - (French) Amiral - Amir - Ruler

Abracadabra - I will create as has been spoken

Adonis - Adon - Lord - Genesis 45:9, Exodus 23:17

Adore - Hadar – To honor, adorn

Agony - Yagon – Sorrow, affliction

After – (Aramaic) Batra - Latter

Albino - Halevanah - Whitening (Frankincense)

Alcove - Kavah - Chamber

Algebra - Chibur - Connect

All - Kol - All

Alley - Aleh - Go up

Alphabet - Alef Bet

Amenable - Amen

Amity - Amit - Neighbor - Leviticus 5:21

Amnesty - Nashi - Cause to forget

An(archy) An(aemic) - Ain - Not

Ancient - Noshen - Old - Leviticus 13:11

Annoy - Ani - Afflict

Antique - Atik - Ancient

Apex - Ofek - Horizon

Arbor - Aravah - Willow

Arch (bishop) Archi(tect) - Orech - Set in order

Area - (Aramaic) Are'a - Land, world

Arithmetic - Rashum - Recorded

Arm - Amah - Arm's length

Arya(n) - Arieh - Lion (The lion is the symbol of Iran)

Ash - Esh - Fire

Ash (Tree) - Eshel - Tamarisk tree

Ashamed - Asham - To be guilty, bear punishment

Asia - Esh - Fire (East - rising of the sun)

Asin(ine) - Aton - Ass

Asp - Sephiphon - Horned snake

At - Ad - Until

Aura - Or - Light - Genesis 1:3

Auxil(iary) - Ozer - To help, assist

Ava(rice) - Avah - Desire

Aviate - Af - Fly

Babble - Bavel - Babel - Genesis 11:9

Bad - Badoot - Fraud, deceit

Ba(l)sam - Bosem - Balm, perfume, fragrance

Ball - Balal - To Blow, swell

Bare - Bi'er - To clear out

Barley - Bar - Cereal - Genesis 42:3

Basil - Bitzel - To flavour, spice (as with onions) - Numbers 11:5

Bat - Bad - Wooden, board, stave - Exodus 25:13

Be - Ba - To come to

Beak(er) - Bakbook - Bucket

Berry - Peri - Fruit - Genesis 1:29

Bet - Betach - Surely, certainly

Bid - Bata - To proclaim, utter

Bleak - Balak - Empty, void and waste - Isaiah 24:1; Nahum 2:11

Bore - Bor - Hole, pit

Boulder - Bolet - Protruding

Brass - Barzel - Iron - Genesis 4:22

Breach - Pritzah - Pierce, prick

Bright - Barak - Glittering, gem, lightning

Bucket - Bakbook

Bur(n) - Bo'ar - Burned - Exodus 3:2

Burst - Peretz - Break through

Butcher - Basar - Meat

By - B

Cab, Cabin, Cave - Koobah - Chamber - Numbers 25:8

Cable - Kevel - Fetter - Psalms 105:18 & 149:8

Cake - Kikar - Loaf - Genesis 20:23

Call - Kol - Noise, voice - Exodus 32:17

Calumny - Kelimah - Insult, shame - Proverbs 28:7

Camel - Gamal - Camel - Genesis 24:10

Capitalism - Chafetz - Wish, desire - Psalms 34:13

Car - Char - Saddle (of camel) - Genesis 31:34

Carob - Charoov - Carob - Talmud Shabbat 33b; Berachot 17b

Carve - Cherev - Sword - Genesis 3:24

Cell - Ke'le - Prison - II Kings 25:27

Chaise - Keis - Seat, throne - Exodus 17:16

Change - Shaneh - To change, alter, differ

Char - Charah - To kindle, burn, to be angry - Numbers 11:33

Character - Charoot - Carved, engraved - Exodus 32:16

Chaste - Chasid - Pious, kind

Checkmate - Sheikh Met - The chief is dead

C(h)er(ish) - Yakar

Cinnamon - Kinamon - Song of Songs 4:14

Circle - Igul

Collar - Ol - Colllar, yoke

Colloss(us) - Galiat (Goliath) - I Samuel 17:4

Common - K'mo - Genesis 41:39

Consult - Sh'eilita - (Aramaic) Inquiry - Daniel 4:16

Coral - Goral - Pebble (lot) - Leviticus 16:8

Core - Ikar - The fundamental, main thing - Leviticus 25:47

Corn - Goral - Grain - Job 39:12

Corner - Cornet - Corn(ucopia) - Unicorn - Keren - Corner, horn, ray

Cosmos - Gashmioot

Cotton - Kootnah - Cotton, coat of many colors - Genesis 37:3

Could - Yechol

Couple - Kafool - Double, (Ma)chpelah (double grave) - Genesis 23:9

Crab - Akrav - Scorpion - I Kings 12:11

Creed - Char'eid - God fearing

Cross - Ker'es - Clasp - Exodus 26:11

Crow - Orev - Crow (Raven)

Cube - Kubiya - Dice cube

Cucumber - Kikayon - Gourd - Jonah 4:6

Cut - Kat

Cypress - Gof'er - Gopher wood - Genesis 6:14

Czar - Sar - Prince, leader - Jeremiah 17:15

Damn - Dan - To judge - Genesis 15:14

Dark - Dalach - Troubled - Ezekiel 32:2

De - Dee - From, of - I Samuel 7:16

(De)cifer - Sefer - Book

Delta - Dalet

Direc(tion) - Derech - Way

Disperse - Paras - Spread out - Deuteronomy 14:7

Div(ine) - Tov - Good

Drip - D'leepah - Leak - Ecclesiates 10:18

Drive - Darvan - A goad (to drive oxen)

Duo - Doo - (Aramaic) Two

Dumb - Domi - Silent - Psalms 62:6

Dye - D'yoo - Ink - Jeremiah 36:18

Each - Echad - One - Genesis 1:5

Earth - Eretz - Earth - Genesis 1:1

Ebony - Hovnee - Ebony - Ezekiel 27:17

Eccel(lent) - Atzil - Noble

Eight - Chet - Eight

Elect - Leket - Gather, glean, pick - Leviticus 19:9

El(k) - Ayal - Stag, hart - Isaiah 35:6

Endow - Nadav - Freewill-offering - Exodus 35:29

En(scon)ce - (yi)shkon - Dwell - Deuteronomy 33:12

Etym(ology) - Emet - Truth

Europe - Ma'arav - West - Psalms 103:12

Eve(ning) - He'ov - Darken, become cloudy - Lamentations 2:1

Evil - Avel - Unrighteousness, injustice - Leviticus 19:25

Exit - Chootz - Outside

Eye - Ayin - Eye - Exodus 21:24

Facul(ty) - Fa'al - Work (of hands) - Deuteronomy 33:11

Fade - Feer - Disappeared, died out - Proverbs 24:22

Fag - Fag - Faint - Genesis 45:26; Habakkuk 1:14; Psalm 38:8

Faith - Betach - Trust - Psalms 13:6

Fall - Nafal - Fall - Exodus 21:33

Fat - Pad(er) - Suet - Leviticus 1:8

Fig - Fageyah - Green figs - Song of Songs 2:13

For - (B')avoor - So that - Genesis 27:4

Frac(tion) - Perek - Fracture, break apart

Free - Farua - Let loose, cast away restraint - Exodus 32:25; II Chronicles 28:11

Fruit - Perot - Fruits

Galbanum - Chelb'nah

Gargle - Girgeir - Throat - Garon - Neck - Garg'rot - Proverbs 3:3

Gaze - Chazah - Perceive, behold - Chozeh - Stargazers - Isaiah 47:13

Gene, Genesis, (Be)gin, Origin - Gan - Garden (of Eden) - Gamete

Giraffe - Garon - Throat

Goad - Chod - Edge, point - Proverbs 27:17

Goblet - Gavia - Goblet - Genesis 44:17

Good - Gad - Good fortune - Genesis 30:11; Isaiah 65:11

Gospel - Sipoor - Recount, tell - Genesis 24:66

Govern - Kiven - To direct, put in place

Grain - Garin - Seed - (Me)gurah - Granary - Haggai 2:19

Graphite - Oferet - Lead - Genesis 15:10

Grap(ple) - (E)grof - Clenched fist (grip)

Grass - Geresh - (generally agricultural (yield) - (Mi)grash - Open space

Groan - Garon - Cry with a full throat - Isaiah 58:1

Ground - Goren - Threshing floor - Joel 2:24

Guerr/illa - Goor - Contend - Deuteronomy 2:9

Gyre - Galgal - Wheel - Ecclesiastes 12:6

Hagi(ographa) - (Greek) Hagi - Holy -
Chag - (Holy) Festival - Exodus 23:15

Hail - Hallel - Praise - Full Hallel - Psalms 113 - 118

Halo - Hilah - Halo, sheen (as in moon or holy man) -
Job 29:3

Hang - Henek - Strangle - Nahum 2:13

Harem - Cherem - To ban, excommunicate -
Leviticus 27:29 - A devoted thing

Harm - Charmah - Destruction, extermination –
Deuteronomy 13:16

Harrow - Cherev - Sword, knife blade or plough -
Genesis 3:24

Health - Chalutz - Make strong - Isaiah 58: 11

Hedonism - Eden - Edna - Pleasure

Herd - Ered - Flock, herd or drove - Genesis 32:17

Hollow - Chalal - Space

Hoof - Akev - Heel - Genesis 25:26

Hook - Chakah - Fish-hook - Job 40:25

Hoot - Heyd - Joyful shouting - Ezekiel 7:7

Horrid - Chareid - Shudder - Genesis 27:33

Horn - Keren - Genesis 22:13

Horus - Che'res - Job 9:6 - Sun

Hurry - Ma'hair - Genesis 18:6

Hyssop - Eyzov - Exodus 12:22

I - Ee - (Kanit)ee - I (have acquired) - Genesis 4:1

Idea - Yedee'a - Knowledge, information

If - Af - Though, nevertheless

Iota - (A small quantity - a jot, dot) - Yod - ʼ

Ire - Charah - To be angry - Genesis 4:6

Is - Yesh - There is - I Samuel 17:46

It - Et - Accusative - Genesis 1:1

Jasper - Yashvay - Exodus 39:13

Jinx - Yonah - Jonah - Jonah 1:12

Jubilate - Yovel - Exodus 19:13, Leviticus 25:10

Jurisdiction - Yosheir - I Kings 9:4

Juxtapose - Yachad - Genesis

Kaiser (Caesar, Czar) - Keter - Crown, authority, rulership

Kernel - Carmel - Groat, hulled kernel - Leviticus 2:14

Khan - Kohein - Priest, leader - Exodus 3:1

Knave - Ganav - Thief - Exodus 20:12

Knock- Nakah - Beat strike - II Samuel 11:15

Lad - Yeled - Boy - Genesis 21:8

Late - Le'at - Slow, sluggish - Isaiah 8:6

Leopard - Lavi - Spotted lion - Genesis 49:9

Lex - (Latin) Law - Lech - Halachah - Genesis 12:1

Lick - Lachak - Lick up - Numbers 22:4

Light - Lahat - Flaming, fiery - Genesis 3:24

Liqu(id) - Lach - Moist - Numbers 6:3

Love - Levah - Emotional attachment - Isaiah 56:6

(L)ute - Ood - Piece of wood - Isaiah 7:4

Macabre - Makabi - Hammer - Isaiah 44:12

Machine - M'chonah - Engine, base - I Kings 7:27-35

Magazine - Machsan - Store

Malign - Ma'al - Wrongdoing - Leviticus 5:15

Mama - Eema - Mother

Mammon – see Money

Man - Ma'an - (Aramaic) Someone, anyone

Manner - Min - Kind, sort, species - Genesis 1:21

Many - Amon - Many

Map - Mapa - Map

Marine (Marinate) - Mar, Mariri - Bitter - Deuteronomy 32:24

Mark(et) - Machar - Sell - Genesis 37:36

Mar(oon) - (French) Marron - Mecheir -
Dark, brownish-red - Job 16:16

Mask - Maskah - Masach - Mask, curtain, covering -
Exodus 26:36

Mass (Latin) massa - Lump, mass - (Greek) maza -
barley cake - Matzot - Unleavened bread - Exodus 8:7

Mat - Mitah - Bed, couch - Genesis 48:2

Me - Ani - I (French) Nous - Anoo - We

Meaning - Ma'an - L'ma'an - For the sake (purpose) of -
Exodus 1:11

Measure - M'sorah - Measure - Leviticus 19:35

Meet - Mo'ed - Meeting - Exodus 30:26

Melo(drama) - Milah - Word, of note - Job 30:9

Meter - Midah - Measure, size, characteristic - Exodus - 26:2

Might - Me'od - Force, strength, might - Deuteronomy 6:5

Minus - M'nat - Part, portion (minute) - Jeremiah 13:25

Mirror - Mar'ah - Mirror- Exodus 38:8

Mix - Mas'chah - Mingled - Proverbs 9:2

Moat - Mot - Obstruction - Psalms 66:9

Mock - Mook - Scoff - Psalm 73:8

Molar - Malal - Rub, scrape, soften

Money - Maneh - Weight, count, money - Ezekiel 45:12

Muck - Mak - Decay, rottenness, rot – Isaiah 5:24

Mus(cle) - Mashak - To pull, extend,
lengthen, draw up - Jeremiah 38:13

Musk - Matok - Sweet, soft, pleasant, juicy -
Song of Songs 2:3

Myrtle - Mor - Myrrh - Exodus 30:23; Psalms 45:8

Myster(y) - Mistar - Secret place - Jeremiah 13:17

Navy - Latin (Navis - Hollowed out [A boat, ship]) -
Navoov - Hollow - Jeremiah 53:21

Neck - Henek - Strangle - Nahum 2:3

New - Noov - To spring forth, to bear fruit - Psalms 92:15

Next - Neged - Against, opposite -
Genesis 2:19; Exodus 19:2; Joshua 5:13

Night - Nachat - Quiet, rest - Isaiah 30:5

No - Noo (infinitive of Hanee) - To disallow - Numbers 30:6

Now - Na – Now - Genesis 12: 11; 18:21; 27:2

Notary - Notar - Watchman, keeper - Song of Songs 1:6

Oath - Ot - Mark of Divine purpose - Genesis 9:13:
Isaiah: 37:30

Obedie(nce) - Avdoot - To serve, be a slave - Genesis 29:18

Obese - Avas - Fatten, stuff - I Kings 5:3

(Ob)scure - Dark, black - Leviticus 13:31

Occur - Kara - To befall, meet up, happen -
Genesis 42:29; 49:1

Ogre - Og - King of Bashan (giant) -
Numbers 21:33; Deuteronomy 3:11

Or - O - Or

Organ - Irgoon - Organization

Or(iole) - Or - Light

Orology (study of mountains) - Har - Mountain

(Ortho)dox (Latin) Right knowledge - De'a - Knowledge, opinion - Leviticus 4:23; Job 32:10; Isaiah 28:9

Over - Avar - Past (in time or grammar)

Pace - Pasa - To march, step - Isaiah 27:4

Pall - Afal - Darkness, gloom, the 9th Plague - Exodus 10:23

Pane(l) - Panim - Face - Genesis 43:31

Part - Prat - Particular, detail - Leviticus 19:10

Patio – Patach - To open wide – Genesis 7:11

Peek - Pikach - Genesis 3:7

Pepper - Pilpel

Pester - Patzar - Urged greatly - Genesis 19:3

Phrase - Lifros - To declare - Leviticus 24:12

Pirate - Paritz - Violent robber - Jeremiah 7:11; Ezekiel 18:10

Pitch - Botz - Mud, mire - Jeremiah 38:22

Plea - Pilel - To entreaty - Psalms 106:30

Plough - Palach - Cleave earth - Psalms 141:7

Preach - Farash - To comment (on), expound

(Pre)cede - Kidem - To come to meet - Psalms 88:14; 95:2

(Pre)pare - Farah - To be fruitful - Hosea 13:15

Press - Paratz - To press, urge

Prize - Pras - To deal, give out, prize - Isaiah 58:7

Prostitute - Pritzoot - Obsenity, licentiousness

Proto(type) - Pe'ter - Firstborn, firstling - Exodus 34:19-20

Quash - Kavash - To master, force, subdue - Genesis 1:28

Query - Che'ker - Inquire, Investigate - Deuteronomy 13:15

Quiet - (She)ket - Quiet, rest - Ruth 3:18

Ram - Re'em - Wild ox - Deuteronomy 33:17

Rattle - Ret'et - To tremble - Jeremiah 49:24

Rave(n) - Orev - Raven - Genesis 8:7

Ravenous - Ra'av - Famine, hunger - Genesis 26:1;
Proverbs 25:21

Reach - Orech - Length - Genesis 6:15

Red - Greek (Rhodon) - Varod - Rose red - Vered - Rose

Reek - Reyach - Fragrance, aroma - Genesis 8:20-21

Regular - Rageel - Usual, normal, habitual

Rife - Rav - Abundance - Exodus 34:6

Rivalry - Reev - Quarrel, dispute, strife - Genesis 13:7

Root - Beginning, head (root) - Genesis 1:1

Rota(te) - Ratza - To run - Genesis 24:29

Ruth(less) - Root - Ruth (pity, compassion)

Sack - Sak - Sack, bag - Leviticus 11:32

Saga - Sichah - Speech, talk, oration - Psalms - 145:5

Sandal - Sandal - Sandal - Yochanan HaSandlar - Pirkey Avot

Samurai - Shomeir - Guardian

Salvation - Shalva (Shalom) - Peace - Psalms 122:7

Sapphire - Sapir - Sapphire - Exodus 39:11

Sash - Sheish - Fine linen - Exodus 28:39

Satrap - Shot'eir - Officer, policeman - Deuteronomy 16:18

Sauce - Assis - Fruit juice - Song of Songs 8:2

Savoir - (Aramaic Savar) - To understand, think

Saw - Masur - Saw - Isaiah 10:15

Scale - Shak'el (Shekel) - To weigh - Genesis 23:16

Scalp - Kleepah - To shell, peel

Scare - Sa'ar - Dread, shudder - Deuteronomy 32:17

S(carf) - Oref - Neck - Leviticus 5:8

Scarlet - Sakar - To paint red - Zechariah 1:8

Sceptre - Shevet - Rod, staff - Isaiah 28:27

School - Eshkol - Bunch, cluster - Numbers 13:23 -
Sechel - Understanding (skill)

Scissors - Guzuz - To shear, clip - Genesis 31:19

(S)coop - Kaf - Ladle - Numbers 7:14

Scope - Shekaf - To face, be seen, look out of - Genesis 26:8

Scour - Shachar - Search, seek - Psalms 78:34; Hosea 5:15

Scruff - Oref - Neck - Leviticus 5:8; Jeremiah 2:27

Seat - Shait - Buttocks - Isaiah 20:4

Secret - (Latin Secretus - Set apart) - Karet - Cut off - Numbers 13:23

Secure - Sa'goor - To close, lock, seclude - Leviticus 13:5; 14:38

Sell - Shalach - To send away - Genesis 44:3; Isaiah 27:10; II Kings 2:2

Semantics - Siman - Sign - Shem - Name - Genesis 2:11

Senile - (Ya)shan

Serf - Saraf - Seraph, attendant, angel - Isaiah 6:2

Series - Shurah - Row, line - Job 24:11

Serpent - Saraph - Serpent - Isaiah 14:29

Serrated - Sarat - Cuttings, gashes - Leviticus 21:5

Set - Shet - Set, appoint - Genesis 41:35

Seven - Shivanah (Sheva) - Seven - Job 42:13

Shack - Sookah - Booth, hut - Leviticus 23:42

Shield - Shelet - Shield - II Samuel 8:7

Shower - Se'ir – Shower - Deuteronomy 32:2

Shriek - Shreekah - Whistling, derisive hooting - I Kings 9:8 - Tzarach - Shout, cry, scream - Isaiah 42:13

Sick - Tzookah - Anguish, distress - Isaiah 30:6; Proverbs 1:27

Side - Tzad - Side - Exodus 25:33

Siege - Si'ag - Fence, hedge - Song of Songs 7:3

Silicon - Sela - Rock - Judges 6:20

Sill - Shool - Rim, margin, hem - Exodus 28:33

Silo - She'ol - Pit, grave - Genesis 37:35; Jonah 2:3

Sign - Tziyon - Mark, signpost - II Kings 23:17

Simulation - Semel - Likeness - Deuteronomy 4:16

Seethe - Zeed - Sod - Genesis 25:29

Sin - Zanah - To go astray, fornicate - Genesis 38:24; Exodus 34:15

Sip - Safah - Lip - I Samuel 1:13 - Sip - Cup - Jeremiah 52:19

Sir - Sar - Chief, leader, minister, ruler, officer - Jeremiah 17:25

Siren - Shirah - Song, poetry - Exodus 15:1

Six - Sheish - Leviticus 23:5

Skep(tic) - Shei'af - A doubter - Psalm 119:113

Skirt - Misgeret - Border, rim - Exodus 25:25

Skull - Goolgolet - Skull, head - Exodus 16:16

Skun(k) - Tzachanah - A smell, stench - Joel 2:20

Slalom - Soolam - Ladder, ramp, stairway - Genesis 28:12

Slough - Shalach - Send off, send away, set free - Exodus 7:16

Sludge - Sheleg - Snow - Exodus 4:6; Jeremiah 18:14

Smite - Hishmeed - To destroy, exterminate -
Shmad - Destroy, cut off - Genesis 34:30

Smug - Samach - Joyful satisfaction - Deuteronomy 16:15

Sneak - Zneekah - Furtive, quick-leaping (lions) -
Deuteronomy 33:22

So - Zo - That - Psalm 132:12

Soak - Sach - To anoint - Ruth 3:3

Sodomy - S'dom - Sodom - Genesis 18:19

Sofa - Safah - Couch, rug - II Samuel 17:28

Solemn - Shalem (Solomon) - Whole, complete

Solve - Shalaf - Loosening, untying, unbuckling - Ruth 4:7

Some - Shoom - Anything, (Aramaic) any

Sore - Tzar - An adversary - Tzarah -
Distress, sorrow, anguish - Genesis 42:21

Sound – Sha'on - Noise - Isaiah 24:8

South - Genesis 1:9 - Tachat - Below, under, beneath

Sow - Zerah - Scatter - Ezekiel 5:2 - Zora
- Sowed, dispersed - Exodus 36:9

Space - Shabbat - Exodus 20:8 - Tashbeet -
Leave out - Ezekiel 36:9; Zechariah 10:9

Sparrow - Tzippor - Bird

Spelt - Shibolet - An ear of corn - Genesis 41:5

Spheres - Sephirot - Genesis 15:5

Spirit - Tzfirah - Whistling (of breath, wind) -
Neshamah - Breath - spiritual breath (Indian) Prana

Spy - Tzeepah - To look - Tzafah -
Keep watch upon, look to - Proverbs 15:3; 31:27

(S)table - Hootzav - Set up, established - Psalms 74:17

Stage - Hitzig - Introduce, present

Steal - Hitzeel - Taken away - Genesis 31:16

Stem - Satam - To stop up, shut, fill, clog - Genesis 26:15

Stone - Tzoonam - Rock, granite, flint

Store - Otzar - Storehouse, treasury - Proverbs 21:20

Strait - Tzarooot - Narrowness, pressing troubles

Stre(et) - Sderot - Avenue, boulevard,
ranks of men - II Chronicles 23:14

Stress - Tzarot - Troubles, narrowness, a tight spot

Stretch - Histara - To stretch oneself out - Isaiah 28:20

Stubborn - Nitzvah - Resoluteness, steadfastness -
Nitzav - Standing - Genesis 18:2

Suffer - Saval - Suffer, endure - Genesis 49:15;
Lamentations 5:7

Suffice - Safak - To be sufficient - I Kings 20:10; Isaiah 2:6;
Job 20:22

Suit - Sute - Garment, suit - Genesis 49:11

Sultan - Shilton - Rule, power, government - Ecclesiastes 8:4

Summit - Tzameret - Summit, top - Ezekiel 17:3; 31:3

Summon - Zimein - To invite

Sun - Shanah - Year (like moon/month) - Deuteronomy 11:12

Super - Shapir - Handsome, elegant, fine, good -
Genesis 49:21

Supper - Safah - To feed - Mispo - Animal food, fodder -
Genesis 24:25

Swivel - S'vivon - Toy top - Sovev -
Turn around - Genesis 42:24; Joshua 6:4

Sycamore - Sik'mah - Sycamore - I Kings 10:27; Psalms 78:47

Syrup - Saraf - To swallow, drink in

Tap - Tav - Mark, sign, musical not - Ezekiel 9:4

Taboo - To'evah - Off limits, proscribed thing - Deuteronomy 7:26

Take - Atak - To remove - Genesis 12:8

Talism(an) - Tzelem - Image - Genesis 1:26; Ezekiel 23:14

Tap - Tofaf - to tap a drum - Psalms 68:26

Taur(us) - Tor - (Aramaic) Bull - (Hebrew) Shor - Deuteronomy 33:17

Team - Te'oom - Twin - Genesis 25:24

Teat - Dad - Breast, nipple - Ezekiel 23:8; Proverbs 5:19

Techn(ical) - Tikoon - To fix, correct - Ecclesiastes 1:15; 7:13

Term - Terem - Boundary in time - Genesis 24:15

Them - Otam - Them - Genesis 1:27

Therapy - T'roofah - Ezekiel 47:12 -
Rafah - To heal, cure - Exodus 15:26

This - Zot - This - Genesis 34:15 - Thus - II Kings 5:4

Thou - Atah - Genesis 23:6

Tiara - Atarah - Crown - Song of Songs 3:11

Tier - Toor - Row, line, column - Exodus 28:17

Too - Too (Aramaic) Further, more, again

Top - Tzipah - Cover, top - Exodus 26:29

Torpor - Toorpah - Weakness - Ezekiel 1:24

Toss - Toose - To fly swiftly - Job 9:26

Toucan - Tooki - Parrot, peacock - I Kings 10:22;
II Chronicles 9:2

Towel - T'vool - Flowing turban – Ezekiel 23:15

Tour - Toor - Exploe (the land) - Numbers 13:2

Track - Darach - Tread, step, march, walk - Joshua 1:3

Trek - Derech - Way, road - Genesis 3:24

Trophy - Teref - Plucked off, torn off - Genesis 8:11;
Proverbs 31:15

Tuna - Tanin - Sea monster, serpent - Genesis 1:21

Twist - Tavah - To spin, twist fibres - Exodus 35:25-26

Ulul(ation) - Y'lal - Howling - Deuteronomy 32:10

(Uni)corn - Keren - Horn - Deuteronomy 33:17

Urge - Errgah - Longing, craving - Ereg -
Crave after, cry for, pant - Psalms 42:2

Use - Assiyah - Doing, acting - Genesis 24:12

Vacate - Bakak - To empty - Isaiah 24:1

Vain - Av'en - Vanity, nothingness - Isaiah 41:29

Van (Dutch) Von (German) - Ben - Offspring - Leviticus 4:3

Vat - Chavit - (Aramaic) Barrel, cask

Veer - Avoor - To go over - I Samuel 14:4

Vent(ricle) - (Latin) Venter - Belly - Genesis 30:2;
I Kings 7:20

Ves(t) - L'voosh - Clothing - Genesis 3:21;Job 24:7;
Esther 6:8

Vet(eran - Vateek - Ancient, old - Ben Sira 36:20 & Talmud

Veto - Vatel - To stop, cease, annul - Ecclesiastes 12:3

Via - Bah; Oovah - To come - Genesis 24:14

Video - Habet - Look! - Genesis 15:5

Vile - Naval - Vile, villain - Isaiah 32:5

Vine - Gefen - Genesis 9:21; Deuteronomy 8:8

Vir(ile) - Gever - A man - Job 38:3 - G'vurah - Strength,
might

Vivid - Aviv - Spring - Exodus 13:4

Voc(alization) - Bocheh; Yavech - To cry - Exodus 2:6;
Genesis 27:38

Vote - Avot - To give or take a pledge - Deuteronomy 24:10

Wallow - Balal - To mix, confuse, stir, knead - Genesis 11:9,

Wail - Aveil - Mourn, grief, howling - Avoy - Woe, alas - Proverbs 23:29

Walk - Halach - To walk - Judges 4:8 - Lech - Go! - Genesis 12:1

Weak - Rach - Soft, tender, weak - Genesis 29:17

Wed - Avot - Pledge - Deuteronomy 24:10

Wheat - Chitah - Wheat - Deuteronomy 8:8

When - Bin - During - Jonah 4:10

Who - Hoo - He, it, this, who - Genesis 4:20

Woe - Avoy - Woe, alas - Proverbs 23:29

Worm - Reema - Worm - Isaiah 14:11; Job 25:6

Wrath - Evrah - Wrath - Isaiah 14:6

Wro(ng) - Ra - Bad - Genesis - 2:17

Xeno(phobia) - Sonay - Foe, enemy - Proverbs 25:21; Genesis 29:33

Yell - Y'lal - Howl - Deuteronomy 32:10

Yet - Od - Still, yet - Ait - A time - Ecclesiastes 1:1

Yoke - Yachad - To join - Genesis 22:8

Young - Yoneik - A suckling child - Numbers 11:12

Zealous - Zareez - Quick, alert

Zircon - Zarchan - Phospherous -
Zerach - To shine - Psalm 112:4

Zodiac - Tzedek - Justice - Leviticus 19:16

We see in Genesis that originally every person in the world spoke the same language, yet God judged them not to be worthy to maintain this then, but now we can keenly look forward to the time when everyone on earth will once again be speaking a language that they will all comprehend.

The vision of the future that is foretold in the promise that God gives in His Torah, and amplified through the words of the Hebrew prophets, is of a harmonious state of existence that will prevail universally following the eventual return of the Children of Israel to their ancient homeland.

The Torah gives us an assurance that when Israel returns and truly becomes 'a light to the nations', all the people of the world will ultimately recognize the Divine within themselves, in each other, in everything and everywhere.

> *"They will neither hurt nor destroy on all My holy mountain, for the earth will be full of the knowledge of God as the waters cover the sea (Isaiah 11:9)."*

At that time, the people of all the nations will be able to understand and commune with each other freely, as the whole world will then, with grateful thanks to God, be enjoying good and moral lives, and will once again be speaking the same language – this time it will be the language of love.

DIVINE ENCRYPTION

The vast edifice in all its aspects that is known as Judaism is founded on the unique phenomenon in human history, which was that God, the Creator of Heaven and Earth, witnessed by the Children of Israel, gave the prophet-leader Moses, the Torah on Mount Sinai.

The rabbis describe the Torah as the blueprint of Creation; all the secrets of the Universe are to be found in it. As Ben Bag Bag says in Ethics of the Fathers 5:25, "Turn it over and over for everything is in it."

Understanding that there is a multi-level of meaning divinely sown into the holy text, helps us in approaching the subject of what has been called the *Torah Codes*. Throughout Jewish history many sages had noted names, messages and teachings encoded in regular patterns in the Torah, among them the Vilna Gaon and the hero and genius Rabbi Michael Dov Weissmandl, but it wasn't until the advent of the computer that the revelation of the astonishing extent of these previously unknown ciphers in the Torah became apparent.

One phenomenon for which no computer is required, is the repetition of a certain word in a section where that word has a particular significance. Just as the number **seven** is of significance in the narration of the first week of Creation, the **seven** days of Pesach (Passover) and Succot (Tabernacles), the **seven** weeks of the Counting of the Omer, between Pesach and Shavuot (Pentecost), the **seven** years to the Shmittah (Sabbatical) year, and the **seven** times **seven** years until the

Yovel (Jubilee) year, so too do we find in numerous places that a word is repeated **seven** times in certain sections, as if the reader is urged to dwell on this sevenfold repetition, just as is found in the following example:

משה עמלק יד - MOSHE AMALEK HAND

Shemot 17:8-16

ח וַיָּבֹא, **עֲמָלֵק**; וַיִּלָּחֶם עִם-יִשְׂרָאֵל, בִּרְפִידִם.

8 Then came **Amalek**, and fought with Israel in Rephidim.

ט וַיֹּאמֶר **מֹשֶׁה** אֶל-יְהוֹשֻׁעַ בְּחַר-לָנוּ אֲנָשִׁים, וְצֵא הִלָּחֵם **בַּעֲמָלֵק**; מָחָר, אָנֹכִי נִצָּב עַל-רֹאשׁ הַגִּבְעָה, וּמַטֵּה הָאֱלֹהִים, בְּיָדִי.

9 And **Moses** said unto Joshua: 'Choose us out men, and go out, fight with **Amalek**; tomorrow I will stand on the top of the hill with the rod of God in my **hand**.'

י וַיַּעַשׂ יְהוֹשֻׁעַ, כַּאֲשֶׁר אָמַר-לוֹ **מֹשֶׁה**--לְהִלָּחֵם, בַּעֲמָלֵק; **וּמֹשֶׁה** אַהֲרֹן וְחוּר, עָלוּ רֹאשׁ הַגִּבְעָה.

10 So Joshua did as **Moses** had said to him, and fought with **Amalek**; and **Moses**, Aaron, and Hur went up to the top of the hill.

יא וְהָיָה, כַּאֲשֶׁר יָרִים **מֹשֶׁה יָדוֹ**--וְגָבַר יִשְׂרָאֵל; וְכַאֲשֶׁר יָנִיחַ **יָדוֹ**, וְגָבַר **עֲמָלֵק**.

11 And it came to pass, when **Moses** held up his **hand**, that Israel prevailed; and when he let down his **hand**, **Amalek** prevailed.

יב וִידֵי **מֹשֶׁה** כְּבֵדִים, וַיִּקְחוּ-אֶבֶן וַיָּשִׂימוּ תַחְתָּיו וַיֵּשֶׁב עָלֶיהָ; וְאַהֲרֹן וְחוּר תָּמְכוּ בְיָדָיו, מִזֶּה אֶחָד וּמִזֶּה אֶחָד, וַיְהִי יָדָיו אֱמוּנָה, עַד-בֹּא הַשָּׁמֶשׁ.

12 But **Moses'** hands were heavy; and they took a stone, and put it under him, and he sat thereon; and Aaron and Hur stayed up his **hand**s, the one on the one side, and the other on the other side; and his **hand**s were steady until the going down of the sun.

יג וַיַּחֲלֹשׁ יְהוֹשֻׁעַ אֶת-**עֲמָלֵק** וְאֶת-עַמּוֹ, לְפִי-חָרֶב.

13 And Joshua discomfited **Amalek** and his people with the edge of the sword.

יד וַיֹּאמֶר יְהוָה אֶל-**מֹשֶׁה**, כְּתֹב זֹאת זִכָּרוֹן בַּסֵּפֶר, וְשִׂים, בְּאָזְנֵי יְהוֹשֻׁעַ: כִּי-מָחֹה אֶמְחֶה אֶת-זֵכֶר **עֲמָלֵק**, מִתַּחַת הַשָּׁמָיִם.

14 And the LORD said unto **Moses**: 'Write this for a memorial in the book, and rehearse it in the ears of Joshua: for I will utterly blot out the remembrance of **Amalek** from under heaven.'

טו וַיִּבֶן **מֹשֶׁה**, מִזְבֵּחַ; וַיִּקְרָא שְׁמוֹ, יְהוָה נִסִּי.

15 And **Moses** built an altar, and called the name of it Adonai-nissi.

טז וַיֹּאמֶר, כִּי-**יָד** עַל-כֵּס יָהּ,

16 And he said: 'The **hand** upon the throne of

126

מִלְחָמָה לַיהוָה, בַּעֲמָלֵק-- the LORD: the LORD will have war with **Amalek** from generation to generation.'
מִדֹּר, דֹּר.

What is even more remarkable is the phenomenon called an *equidistant letter sequence (ELS)*. Right at the start of the Torah, in the first portion called Bereishit (in the beginning), we can find Avraham (Abraham) and Yisrael (Israel-Jacob) in such sequences of equally distanced intervals between letters.

Firstly, with respect to Avraham, the man who brought the knowledge of the one true God to the world, we find his name encoded in the very first chapter of the Torah. Here is how we find his name. When we look at the narrative of the creation of living beings on the fifth day, and from the **Aleph** of the first letter of the name of God in verse 22 we count 50 letters, we will find **Veit**, and 50 letters gives **Reish** and 50 letters – **Heh** and 50 letters – **Mem**, we discover the name **Avraham** spelled out, with the final letter being also the final letter of the name of God in verse 26!

It is little wonder that **Israel** is also to be discovered within the first chapter of the Torah, as it was taught by the rabbis that the people of Israel were already in God's "thoughts" prior to the creation of Heaven and Earth. This is commented on by Rabbi Shlomo Riskin where he notes that, "The sacred Zohar teaches that God, the nation of Israel and the Torah are one. This suggests that God may be experienced through those phenomena that are also perceived to be eternal. Since Israel is eternal [by Divine oath, Genesis 15] and since the Torah is eternal, God, Israel and the Torah are inextricably linked by common eternity."

Amazingly, the hidden name of Israel begins at the very last letter of the description of the Creation, culminating in the creation of mankind. At the end of the sixth day, just before the first Shabbat, when God "finished His work which He had made and rested" is described, we see the letter Yud – the last letter of Yom HaShishi (the sixth day). Now (just as we find ourselves going into the **seven**th day), we count **seven** letters. We then count another **seven** letters and **seven** letters and **seven** letters, and we have spelled out **Yisrael** (Israel)!

Incidentally, Israel is also to be discovered in the same section, encoded in reverse, at an even interval of 50, perfectly symmetrically, with the middle letter (Reish) being the **same** letter that we saw as the middle letter when we counted in a forward direction!

As the Torah was given to the Children of Israel via the hands of Moshe (Moses), it would be fitting if we could find in Bereishit, the first portion of the Torah, some reference to him. So it comes as little surprise, yet still with a great deal of amazement, to discover a clear allusion to Moses in the final chapter of this portion.

In Genesis 6:3 it reads, And the Lord said, "My spirit shall not abide in man forever, for that he also is flesh; therefore shall his days be a hundred and twenty years." Now, to most students of the Torah, if you would ask them, "Who in the

Torah lived to one hundred and twenty? They would immediately answer, "Moshe." Indeed, in the Torah, Moses is the only person who is recorded as having lived to this age. When we look at this verse again, we find a very unusual word to describe "for that", and that word is *b'shagam.*

This is the hint regarding Moses. If we use *gematria,* (letter value – where Aleph the first letter equals one, Beit the second letter 2...), we discover that the word ***b'shagam*** consists of four letters – **Beit**, **Shin**, **Gimmel** and **Mem**, which added together equals 2 + 300 + 3 + 40 = 345. This word (*b'shagam*) occurs in the sentence where we read, "...shall his days be a hundred and twenty" (a number uniquely found in the Torah only regarding Moshe's age). Now, if we then look at the name of **Moshe** (Moses), which is made up of the letters **Mem**, **Shin** and **Heh**, corresponding to forty plus three hundred plus five – this also equals 345. So, in the very first portion of the Torah, in the only sentence in the Five Books of Moses that mentions one hundred and twenty years (other than the one actually mentioning the age of Moses), we find a clear allusion to Moses!

Equidistant Letter Sequence

Words discovered at equidistant letter intervals emerge in a considerable number of cases, very close to the same word or concept as it appears in the simple reading of the text.

Many of the most prominent of these effects are in relation to extremely rare words or words that appear only once in the Torah.

In the following, the word where the first letter is found is indicated, then the interval between the letters is given:

HEBREW NAMES FOR THE FIVE BOOKS OF MOSES

Genesis - Bereishit * Exodus - Shemot * Leviticus - Vayikra

Numbers - Bamidbar * Deuteronomy - Devarim

גביע - GOBLET

(in the section that speaks about the goblet)

Bereishit 44:11-13 בג‌דול v.12 interval 8

יא וַיְמַהֲרוּ, וַיּוֹרִדוּ אִישׁ אֶת-אַמְתַּחְתּוֹ-- אָרְצָה; וַיִּפְתְּחוּ, אִישׁ אַמְתַּחְתּוֹ.

11 Then they hastened, and took down every man his sack to the ground, and opened every man his sack.

יב וַיְחַפֵּשׂ--בַּגָּדוֹל הֵחֵל, וּבַקָּטֹן כִּלָּה; וַיִּמָּצֵא, הַגָּבִיעַ,* בְּאַמְתַּחַת, בִּנְיָמִן.

12 And he searched, beginning at the eldest, and leaving off at the youngest; and the goblet was found in Benjamin's sack.

יג וַיִּקְרְעוּ, שִׂמְלֹתָם; וַיַּעֲמֹס אִישׁ עַל-חֲמֹרוֹ, וַיָּשֻׁבוּ הָעִירָה.

13 And they rent their clothes, and laded every man his ass, and returned to the city.

בעננִי - IN THE CLOUDS OF

Bereishit 9:11-15 וּבֵין v.13 interval 19

יא וַהֲקִמֹתִי אֶת-בְּרִיתִי אִתְּכֶם, וְלֹא-יִכָּרֵת כָּל-בָּשָׂר עוֹד מִמֵּי הַמַּבּוּל; וְלֹא-יִהְיֶה עוֹד מַבּוּל, לְשַׁחֵת הָאָרֶץ.

11 And I will establish My covenant with you; neither shall all flesh be cut off any more by the waters of the flood; neither shall there any more be a flood to destroy the earth.'

יב וַיֹּאמֶר אֱלֹהִים, זֹאת אוֹת-הַבְּרִית אֲשֶׁר-אֲנִי נֹתֵן בֵּינִי וּבֵינֵיכֶם, וּבֵין כָּל-נֶפֶשׁ חַיָּה, אֲשֶׁר אִתְּכֶם--לְדֹרֹת, עוֹלָם.

12 And God said: 'This is the token of the covenant which I make between Me and you and every living creature that is with you, for perpetual generations:

יג אֶת-קַשְׁתִּי, נָתַתִּי בֶּעָנָן; וְהָיְתָה לְאוֹת בְּרִית, בֵּינִי וּבֵין הָאָרֶץ.

13 I have set My bow in the cloud, and it shall be for a token of a covenant between Me and the earth.

יד וְהָיָה, *בְּעַנְנִי* עָנָן עַל-הָאָרֶץ, וְנִרְאֲתָה הַקֶּשֶׁת, בֶּעָנָ**ן**.

14 And it shall come to pass, when I bring clouds over the earth, and the bow is seen in the cloud,

טו וְזָכַרְתִּי אֶת-בְּרִיתִי, אֲשֶׁר בֵּי**נִ**י וּבֵינֵיכֶם, וּבֵין כָּל-נֶפֶשׁ חַ**יָּ**ה, בְּכָל-

15 that I will remember My covenant, which is between Me and you and every living creature of all

בָּשָׂר ; וְלֹא-יִהְיֶה עוֹד הַמַּיִם לְמַבּוּל, לְשַׁחֵת כָּל-בָּשָׂר.

flesh; and the waters shall no more become a flood to destroy all flesh.

לאה רחל - LEAH RACHEL

(in the section mentioning Jacob finding a wife
and in the order that he married them)

Bereishit 28:1-6 קום לך (50) פדנה ארם (50)

א וַיִּקְרָא יִצְחָק אֶל-יַעֲקֹב, וַיְבָרֶךְ אֹתוֹ ; וַיְצַוֵּהוּ וַיֹּאמֶר לוֹ, לֹא-תִקַּח אִשָּׁה מִבְּנוֹת כְּנָעַן.

1 And Isaac called Jacob, and blessed him, and charged him, and said unto him: 'Thou shalt not take a wife of the daughters of Canaan.

ב קוּם לֵךְ פַּדֶּנָה אֲרָם, בֵּיתָה בְתוּאֵל אֲבִי אִמֶּךָ ; וְקַח-לְךָ מִשָּׁם אִשָּׁה, מִבְּנוֹת לָבָן אֲחִי אִמֶּךָ.

2 Arise, go to Paddan-aram, to the house of Bethuel thy mother's father; and take thee a wife from thence of the daughters of Laban thy mother's brother.

ג וְאֵל שַׁדַּי יְבָרֵךְ אֹתְךָ, וְיַפְרְךָ וְיַרְבֶּךָ ; וְהָיִיתָ, לִקְהַל עַמִּים.

3 And God Almighty bless thee, and make thee fruitful, and multiply thee, that thou mayest be a congregation of peoples;

ד וְיִתֶּן-לְךָ אֶת-בִּרְכַּת אַבְרָהָם, לְךָ וּלְזַרְעֲךָ אִתָּךְ--לְרִשְׁתְּךָ אֶת-אֶרֶץ

4 and give thee the blessing of Abraham, to thee, and to thy seed with thee; that thou mayest inherit the land

132

מִגֻרֶיךָ, אֲשֶׁר-נָתַן אֱלֹהִים לְאַבְרָהָם.

of thy sojournings, which God gave unto Abraham.'

ה וַיִּשְׁלַח יִצְחָק אֶת-יַעֲקֹב, וַיֵּלֶךְ פַּדֶּנָה אֲרָ‌ם-אֶל-לָבָן בֶּן-בְּתוּאֵל, הָאֲרַמִּי, אֲחִי רִבְקָה, אֵם יַעֲקֹב וְעֵשָׂו.

5 And Isaac sent away Jacob; and he went to Paddan-aram unto Laban, son of Bethuel the Aramean, the brother of Rebekah, Jacob's and Esau's mother.

ו וַיַּרְא עֵשָׂו, כִּי-בֵרַךְ יִצְחָק אֶת-יַעֲקֹב, וְשִׁלַּח אֹתוֹ פַּדֶּנָה אֲרָם, לָקַחַת-לוֹ מִשָּׁם אִשָּׁה : בְּבָרְכוֹ אֹתוֹ--וַיְצַו עָלָיו לֵאמֹר, לֹא-תִקַּח אִשָּׁה מִבְּנוֹת כְּנָעַן.

6 Now Esau saw that Isaac had blessed Jacob and sent him away to Paddan-aram, to take him a wife from thence; and that as he blessed him he gave him a charge, saying: 'Thou shalt not take a wife of the daughters of Canaan';

מתתיהו - MATITIYAHU

(at the end of the Five Books of Moses, hinting at the final festival of Chanukah)

Devarim 34:5-12 וימת ש**ם** משה (2nd mem) interval 50

ה וַיָּמָת שָׁ**ם** מֹשֶׁה עֶבֶד-יְהוָה, בְּאֶרֶץ מוֹאָב--עַל-פִּי יְהוָה.

5 So Moses the servant of the LORD died there in the land of Moab, according to the word of the LORD.

133

ו וַיִּקְבֹּר אֹתוֹ בַגַּי בְּאֶרֶץ מוֹאָב, מוּל בֵּית פְּעוֹר; וְלֹא-יָדַע אִישׁ אֶת-קְבֻרָתוֹ, עַד הַיּוֹם הַזֶּה.

6 And he was buried in the valley in the land of Moab over against Beth-peor; and no man knoweth of his sepulchre unto this day.

ז וּמֹשֶׁה, בֶּן-מֵאָה וְעֶשְׂרִים שָׁנָה--בְּמֹתוֹ; לֹא-כָהֲתָה עֵינוֹ, וְלֹא-נָס לֵחֹה.

7 And Moses was a hundred and twenty years old when he died: his eye was not dim, nor his natural force abated.

ח וַיִּבְכּוּ בְנֵי יִשְׂרָאֵל אֶת-מֹשֶׁה בְּעַרְבֹת מוֹאָב, שְׁלֹשִׁים יוֹם; וַיִּתְּמוּ, יְמֵי בְכִי אֵבֶל מֹשֶׁה.

8 And the children of Israel wept for Moses in the plains of Moab thirty days; so the days of weeping in the mourning for Moses were ended.

ט וִיהוֹשֻׁעַ בִּן-נוּן, מָלֵא רוּחַ חָכְמָה--כִּי-סָמַךְ מֹשֶׁה אֶת-יָדָיו, עָלָיו; וַיִּשְׁמְעוּ אֵלָיו בְּנֵי-יִשְׂרָאֵל וַיַּעֲשׂוּ, כַּאֲשֶׁר צִוָּה יְהוָה אֶת-מֹשֶׁה.

9 And Joshua the son of Nun was full of the spirit of wisdom; for Moses had laid his hands upon him; and the children of Israel hearkened unto him, and did as the LORD commanded Moses.

י וְלֹא-קָם נָבִיא עוֹד בְּיִשְׂרָאֵל, כְּמֹשֶׁה, אֲשֶׁר יְדָעוֹ יְהוָה, פָּנִים אֶל-פָּנִים.

10 And there hath not arisen a prophet since in Israel like unto Moses, whom the LORD knew face to face;

יא לְכָל-הָאֹתֹת
וְהַמּוֹפְתִים, אֲשֶׁר שְׁלָחוֹ
יְהוָה, לַעֲשׂוֹת, בְּאֶרֶץ
מִצְרָיִם--לְפַרְעֹה וּלְכָל-
עֲבָדָיו, וּלְכָל-אַרְצוֹ.

11 in all the signs and the wonders, which the LORD sent him to do in the land of Egypt, to Pharaoh, and to all his servants, and to all his land;

יב וּלְכֹל הַיָּד הַחֲזָקָה,
וּלְכֹל הַמּוֹרָא הַגָּדוֹל,
אֲשֶׁר עָשָׂה מֹשֶׁה, לְעֵינֵי
כָּל-יִשְׂרָאֵל.

12 and in all the mighty hand, and in all the great terror, which Moses wrought in the sight of all Israel.

THE SEVEN SPECIES - המינים

Within the whole section beginning with Bereishit 1:29 "And God said, 'Behold I have given you every herb yielding seed…" and then the placing of man in the Garden of Eden, until "but of the tree of the knowledge of good and evil, you shall not eat of it…" Bereishit 2:1, are hidden all the Seven Species that are special to the Land of Israel, encoded at equal intervals:

BARLEY - שערה

from Bereishit 1:29 אשר interval -28

WHEAT - חטה

from Bereishit 2:7 היה interval 5

135

WINE - יין

from Bereishit 2:10 ראשים interval -11

DATE - תמר

from Bereishit 2:10 את-הגן interval 5

OLIVE - זית

from Bereishit 2:11 הזהב interval -9

FIG - תאנה

from Bereishit 2:14 פרת interval 14

POMEGRANATE - רמון

from Bereishit 2:17 ורע interval 8

Describing Eden, in 15 verses (Bereishit 2:7-3:3),
there are encoded in equidistant intervals
25 species that grow from the ground!

WHEAT - חטה

Bereishit 2:7 חיה 5

VINE - גפן

Bereishit 2:8 גן -18

GRAPE - ענב

6- הד**ע**ת Bereishit 2:9

CHESTNUT - ערמון

44 הד**ע**ת Bereishit 2:9

DENSE FOREST - עבת

3- ור**ע** Bereishit 2:17

DATE - תמר

5 א**ת**-הגן Bereishit 2:10

ACACIA - שטה

3- **ש**ם Bereishit 2:12

BRAMBLE - אטד

7 ה**א**רץ Bereishit 2:12

CEDAR - ארז

5- ההו**א** Bereishit 2:12

PEANUT - בטן

13 הזה**ב** Bereishit 2:11

FIG - תאנה

Bereishit 2:14 **פרת** 14

WILLOW - ערבה

15- **על**-האדם Bereishit 2:16

POMEGRANATE - רמון

Bereishit 2:17 ו**ר**ע 8

ALOE - אהלים

Bereishit 2:18 וי**א**מר 6

TAMARISK - אשל

2 **א**עשה-לו Bereishit 2:18

OAK - אלון

Bereishit 2:19 ו**א**ת 17

POPLAR - לבנה

85- כ**ל**-חית Bereishit 2:19

CASSIA - קדה

7 י**ק**רא-לו Bereishit 2:19

ALMOND - שקד

5 **שׁ**מו Bereishit 2:19

MASTIC - אלה

2- הָ**א**דם Bereishit 2:21

THORN BUSH - סנה

9 ויּ**ס**גר Bereishit 2:21

HAZEL - לוז

13- על-**ל**האדם Bereishit 2:21

OLIVE - זית

3 יעזב-**ז**איש Bereishit 2:24

ETROG - הדר

3- ויּ**ה**ו Bereishit 2:25

FIR - גפר

8 עץ-ה**ג**ן Bereishit 3:2

THE MENORAH OF THE TORAH

HAROT	HAROT	GOD	TORAH	TORAH
הרות	הרות	י-הוה	תורה	תורה
DEUTERONOMY	NUMBERS	LEVITICUS	EXODUS	GENESIS
דברים	במדבר	ויקרא	שמות	בראשית
				1
1	1	1	1	
	1	1	1	1
1	1	1	1	1
	1	1	1	1
	1	1	1	
		1		

From the 1st ת of the 1st two books, a repeated interval of 50 letters spells תורה TORAH

From the ה of משה, at the beginning of the 4th book, a repeated interval of 50 letters spells הרות HAROT

From the first ה of התורה in the 5th verse of the 5th book, a repeated interval of 49 letters spells הרות HAROT

From the first י of the middle book, a repeated interval of 8 letters spells י-הוה GOD

140

AHARON - אהרן

Vayikra 1:1-13 In this section describing the priestly functions performed by the Priests (Kohanim), the name of Aaron (Aharon), the High Priest (Kohen Gadol) is encoded 25 times at equal intervals in this passage containing 716 letters!

The chances of that happening randomly are 400,000:1

FORETELLING THE FUTURE

WOOD and STONE - עץ ואבן

Devarim 29:15-17

their idols of wood (the Cross)
and stone (the Kaaba…)"

CROSS CRESCENT - צלב סהר

Devarim 29:15-17 מצרים interval 50 כסף interval 50

(The Vilna Gaon says this refers to
[Esav] Christianity and [Yishmael] Islam)

טו כִּי-אַתֶּם יְדַעְתֶּם, אֵת אֲשֶׁר-יָשַׁבְנוּ בְּאֶרֶץ מִצְרָיִם, וְאֵת אֲשֶׁר-עָבַרְנוּ בְּקֶרֶב הַגּוֹיִם, אֲשֶׁר עֲבַרְתֶּם.

15 for ye know how we dwelt in the land of Egypt; and how we came through the midst of the nations through which ye passed;

טז וַתִּרְאוּ, אֶת-

16 and ye have seen

שְׁקוּצֵיהֶם, וְאֵת,
גִּלֻּלֵיהֶם--עֵץ וָאֶבֶן,
כֶּסֶף וְזָהָב אֲשֶׁר עִמָּהֶם.

their detestable things, and their idols, wood and stone, silver and gold, which were with them--

יז פֶּן-יֵשׁ בָּכֶם אִישׁ אוֹ-
אִשָּׁה אוֹ מִשְׁפָּחָה אוֹ-
שֵׁבֶט, אֲשֶׁר לְבָבוֹ פֹנֶה
הַיּוֹם מֵעִם יְהוָה
אֱלֹהֵינוּ, לָלֶכֶת לַעֲבֹד,
אֶת-אֱלֹהֵי הַגּוֹיִם
הָהֵם : פֶּן-יֵשׁ בָּכֶם,
שֹׁרֶשׁ פֹּרֶה רֹאשׁ--
וְלַעֲנָה.

17 lest there should be among you man, or woman, or family, or tribe, whose heart turneth away this day from the LORD our God, to go to serve the gods of those nations; lest there should be among you a root that beareth gall and wormwood;

MAIMONIDES (RAMBAM) and the MISHNEH TORAH
(a book enumerating the 613 commandments in the Torah)

Shemot 11:9 "…that My wonders be multiplied in Egypt"

Both Moshe Rabbeinu and Moshe ben Maimon (Rambam) performed wonders in the land of Egypt.

From the מ of משה in Shemot 11:9 a repeated interval of 50 letters spells **Mishneh** (משנה). Then there is an interval of **613** letters to the second ה of והיה in Shemot 12:13, the final letter of another repeated interval of 50 letters that spells **Torah** (תורה).

142

ט וַיֹּאמֶר יְהוָה אֶל-
מֹשֶׁה, לֹא-יִשְׁמַע אֲלֵיכֶם
פַּרְעֹה--לְמַעַן רְבוֹת
מוֹפְתַי, בְּאֶרֶץ מִצְרָיִם.

9 And the LORD said unto Moses: 'Pharaoh will not hearken unto you; that My wonders may be multiplied in the land of Egypt.'

י וּמֹשֶׁה וְאַהֲרֹן, עָ**שׂ**וּ
אֶת-כָּל-הַמֹּפְתִים
הָאֵלֶּה--לִפְנֵי פַרְעֹה;
וַיְחַזֵּק יְהוָה אֶת-לֵב
פַּרְעֹה, וְלֹא-שִׁלַּח אֶת-
בְּ**נֵ**י-יִשְׂרָאֵל מֵאַרְצוֹ.

10 And Moses and Aaron did all these wonders before Pharaoh; and the LORD hardened Pharaoh's heart, and he did not let the children of Israel go out of his land.

Exodus Chapter 12 שְׁמוֹת

א וַיֹּאמֶר יְהוָה אֶל-
מֹשֶׁה וְאֶל-אַהֲרֹן, בְּאֶרֶץ
מִצְרַיִם לֵאמֹר.

1 And the LORD spoke unto Moses and Aaron in the land of Egypt, saying:

ב הַחֹדֶשׁ **הַ**זֶּה לָכֶם,
רֹאשׁ חֳדָשִׁים: רִאשׁוֹן
הוּא לָכֶם, לְחָדְשֵׁי
הַשָּׁנָה.

2 'This month shall be unto you the beginning of months; it shall be the first month of the year to you.

ג דַּבְּרוּ, אֶל-כָּל-עֲדַת
יִשְׂרָאֵל לֵאמֹר, בֶּעָשֹׂר,
לַחֹדֶשׁ הַזֶּה: וְיִקְחוּ
לָהֶם, אִישׁ שֶׂה

3 Speak ye unto all the congregation of Israel, saying: In the tenth day of this month they shall take to them every man a lamb,

143

לְבֵית-אָבֹת--שֶׂה לַבָּיִת.

according to their fathers' houses, a lamb for a household;

ד וְאִם-יִמְעַט הַבַּיִת, מִהְיוֹת מִשֶּׂה--וְלָקַח הוּא וּשְׁכֵנוֹ הַקָּרֹב אֶל-בֵּיתוֹ, בְּמִכְסַת נְפָשֹׁת: אִישׁ לְפִי אָכְלוֹ, תָּכֹסּוּ עַל-הַשֶּׂה.

4 and if the household be too little for a lamb, then shall he and his neighbour next unto his house take one according to the number of the souls; according to every man's eating ye shall make your count for the lamb.

ה שֶׂה תָמִים זָכָר בֶּן-שָׁנָה, יִהְיֶה לָכֶם; מִן-הַכְּבָשִׂים וּמִן-הָעִזִּים, תִּקָּחוּ.

5 Your lamb shall be without blemish, a male of the first year; ye shall take it from the sheep, or from the goats;

ו וְהָיָה לָכֶם לְמִשְׁמֶרֶת, עַד אַרְבָּעָה עָשָׂר יוֹם לַחֹדֶשׁ הַזֶּה; וְשָׁחֲטוּ אֹתוֹ, כֹּל קְהַל עֲדַת-יִשְׂרָאֵל--בֵּין הָעַרְבָּיִם.

6 and ye shall keep it unto the fourteenth day of the same month; and the whole assembly of the congregation of Israel shall kill it at dusk.

ז וְלָקְחוּ, מִן-הַדָּם, וְנָתְנוּ עַל-שְׁתֵּי הַמְּזוּזֹת, וְעַל-הַמַּשְׁקוֹף--עַל, הַבָּתִּים, אֲשֶׁר-יֹאכְלוּ אֹתוֹ, בָּהֶם.

7 And they shall take of the blood, and put it on the two side-posts and on the lintel, upon the houses wherein they shall eat it.

ח וְאָכְלוּ אֶת-הַבָּשָׂר,

8 And they shall eat the flesh

144

בַּלַּיְלָה הַזֶּה : צְלִי-אֵשׁ וּמַצּוֹת, עַל-מְרֹרִים יֹאכְלֻהוּ.

in that night, roast with fire, and unleavened bread; with bitter herbs they shall eat it.

ט אַל-תֹּאכְלוּ מִמֶּנּוּ נָא, וּבָשֵׁל מְבֻשָּׁל בַּמָּיִם : כִּי אִם-צְלִי-אֵשׁ, רֹאשׁוֹ עַל-כְּרָעָיו וְעַל-קִרְבּוֹ.

9 Eat not of it raw, nor sodden at all with water, but roast with fire; its head with its legs and with the inwards thereof.

י וְלֹא-תוֹתִירוּ מִמֶּנּוּ, עַד-בֹּקֶר ; וְהַנֹּתָר מִמֶּנּוּ עַד-בֹּקֶר, בָּאֵשׁ תִּשְׂרֹפוּ.

10 And ye shall let nothing of it remain until the morning; but that which remaineth of it until the morning ye shall burn with fire.

יא וְכָכָה, תֹּאכְלוּ אֹתוֹ- -מָתְנֵיכֶם חֲגֻרִים, נַעֲלֵיכֶם בְּרַגְלֵיכֶם וּמַקֶּלְכֶם בְּיֶדְכֶם ; וַאֲכַלְתֶּם אֹתוֹ בְּחִפָּזוֹן, פֶּסַח הוּא לַיהוָה.

11 And thus shall ye eat it: with your loins girded, your shoes on your feet, and your staff in your hand; and ye shall eat it in haste--it is the LORD'S passover.

יב וְעָבַרְתִּי בְאֶרֶץ- מִצְרַיִם, בַּלַּיְלָה הַזֶּה, וְהִכֵּיתִי כָל-בְּכוֹר בְּאֶרֶץ מִצְרַיִם, מֵאָדָם וְעַד- בְּהֵמָה ; וּבְכָל-אֱלֹהֵי מִצְרַיִם אֶעֱשֶׂה שְׁפָטִים, אֲנִי יְהוָה.

12 For I will go through the land of Egypt in that night, and will smite all the first-born in the land of Egypt, both man and beast; and against all the gods of Egypt I will execute judgments: I am the LORD.

יג **וְהָיָה** הַדָּם לָכֶם לְאֹת, עַל הַבָּתִּים אֲשֶׁר אַתֶּם שָׁם, וְרָאִיתִי אֶת-הַדָּם, וּפָסַחְתִּי עֲלֵכֶם; וְלֹא-יִהְיֶה בָכֶם נֶגֶף לְמַשְׁחִית, בְּהַכֹּתִי בְּאֶרֶץ מִצְרָיִם.

13 And the blood shall be to you for a token upon the houses where ye are; and when I see the blood, I will pass over you, and there shall no plague be upon you to destroy you, when I smite the land of Egypt.

So, hidden in this section, is an allusion to the Mishneh Torah, written by the Rambam in Egypt expounding on all the 613 commandments in the Torah.

Astonishingly, in this section of the Torah that appears to also refer to Maimonides (the Rambam) and his major work, the Mishneh Torah, we also find mention of the 14th day of the month of Nissan – the birthday of Maimonides!

THE HOLOCAUST (HaShoah)

"Then My anger will flare up against them and I will abandon them, and hide My face from them, they shall be ready prey; and many evils and troubles shall befall them. And they shall say, 'surely it is because our God is not in our midst that these evils have befallen us.' Yet I shall keep My face hidden on that day because of all the evil they have done in turning to other gods" Devarim 31:17-18.

HASHOAH - השואה

Devarim 31:16-19 משה interval 50

טז וַיֹּאמֶר יְהֹוָה אֶל- 16 And the LORD said unto Moses: 'Behold, thou art about to sleep with thy fathers; and this people will rise up, and go astray after the foreign gods of the land, whither they go to be among them, and will forsake Me, and break My covenant which I have made with them.

מֹשֶׁה, הִנְּךָ שֹׁכֵב עִם-
אֲבֹתֶיךָ ; וְקָם הָעָם הַזֶּה
וְזָנָה אַחֲרֵי אֱלֹהֵי נֵכַר-
הָאָרֶץ, אֲשֶׁר הוּא בָא-
שָׁמָּה בְּקִרְבּוֹ, וַעֲזָבַנִי,
וְהֵפֵר אֶת-בְּרִיתִי אֲשֶׁר
כָּרַתִּי אִתּוֹ.

יז וְחָרָה אַפִּי בוֹ בַיּוֹם- 17 Then My anger shall be kindled against them in that day, and I will forsake them, and I will hide My face from them, and they shall be devoured, and many evils and troubles shall come upon them; so that they will say in that day: Are not these evils come upon us because our God is not among us?

הַהוּא וַעֲזַבְתִּים
וְהִסְתַּרְתִּי פָנַי מֵהֶם,
וְהָיָה לֶאֱכֹל, וּמְצָאֻהוּ
רָעוֹת רַבּוֹת, וְצָרוֹת ;
וְאָמַר, בַּיּוֹם הַהוּא,
הֲלֹא עַל כִּי-אֵין אֱלֹהַי
בְּקִרְבִּי, מְצָאוּנִי הָרָעוֹת
הָאֵלֶּה.

יח וְאָנֹכִי, הַסְתֵּר 18 And I will surely hide My face in that day for all the evil which they shall have wrought, in that they are turned unto other gods.

אַסְתִּיר פָּנַי בַּיּוֹם
הַהוּא, עַל כָּל-הָרָעָה,
אֲשֶׁר עָשָׂה : כִּי פָנָה,
אֶל-אֱלֹהִים אֲחֵרִים.

147

HAMAN'S SONS - THE NAZI LEADERS

In the 9th chapter of the Megillah (the Scroll of Esther that is read at Purim), in the place where the ten sons of Haman (who set out to annihilate the Jews) who are about to be hung are listed vertically, there are written next to their names three small letters that were mysteriously placed there.
These small letters ת ש ז spell out the year תש"ז (5)707.

At the Nuremberg War Crimes Tribunal, they were supposed to hang eleven Nazi leaders, but Göring committed suicide before, leaving ten. In fact, when one of the ten who were to be hanged, Julius Streicher, the founder and publisher of the virulent anti-Semitic Nazi newspaper *Der Stürmer,* heard the death penalty pronounced, he shouted "Purimfest 1946!"

They were hanged on October 16th 1946 –
Hoshanah Rabbah **5707**.

THE JEWISH PEOPLE ALREADY HIDDEN IN THE BEGINNING

As previously mentioned, Abraham (Avraham) and Israel (Yisrael) are encoded, and Moses (Moshe) is alluded to right at the beginning of the Torah.

AVRAHAM - אברהם

The first Avraham that is to be found with equidistant intervals, occurs just where the creation of living beings is described.

Notably, for the man who is known for introducing God as our Creator and Sustainer to humanity, it is fitting that this first encoded Avraham begins and ends with the word –

God (א-להים)

Bereishit 1:22 א-להים interval 50

22 And God blessed them, saying: 'Be fruitful, and multiply, and fill the waters in the seas, and let fowl multiply in the earth.'	**כב** וַיְבָרֶךְ אֹתָם אֱלֹהִים, לֵאמֹר: פְּרוּ וּרְבוּ, וּמִלְאוּ אֶת-הַמַּיִם בַּיַּמִּים, וְהָעוֹף, יִרֶב בָּאָרֶץ.
23 And there was evening and there was morning, a fifth day.	**כג** וַיְהִי-עֶרֶב וַיְהִי-בֹקֶר, יוֹם חֲמִישִׁי.
24 And God said: 'Let the earth bring forth the living creature after its kind, cattle, and creeping thing, and beast of the earth after its kind.' And it was so.	**כד** וַיֹּאמֶר אֱלֹהִים, תּוֹצֵא הָאָרֶץ נֶפֶשׁ חַיָּה לְמִינָהּ, בְּהֵמָה וָרֶמֶשׂ וְחַיְתוֹ-אֶרֶץ, לְמִינָהּ; וַיְהִי-כֵן.
25 And God made the beast of the earth after its kind, and the cattle after their kind, and every thing that creepeth upon the ground after its kind; and God saw that it was good.	**כה** וַיַּעַשׂ אֱלֹהִים אֶת-חַיַּת הָאָרֶץ לְמִינָהּ, וְאֶת-הַבְּהֵמָה לְמִינָהּ, וְאֵת כָּל-רֶמֶשׂ הָאֲדָמָה, לְמִינֵהוּ; וַיַּרְא אֱלֹהִים, כִּי-טוֹב.

כו וַיֹּאמֶר אֱלֹהִים, נַעֲשֶׂה אָדָם בְּצַלְמֵנוּ כִּדְמוּתֵנוּ; וְיִרְדּוּ בִדְגַת הַיָּם וּבְעוֹף הַשָּׁמַיִם, וּבַבְּהֵמָה וּבְכָל-הָאָרֶץ, וּבְכָל-הָרֶמֶשׂ, הָרֹמֵשׂ עַל-הָאָרֶץ.

26 And God said: 'Let us make man in our image, after our likeness; and let them have dominion over the fish of the sea, and over the fowl of the air, and over the cattle, and over all the earth, and over every creeping thing that creepeth upon the earth.'

Notice how the first time that the name of Abraham (Avraham) is found encoded in the Torah, the spelling of his name finishes precisely at the moment that God speaks about creating mankind (serving to emphasize the critical importance of the role of this man for all humanity).

This is totally in accord with what God revealed to Abraham in Genesis 12:3 saying, "… and in you shall all the families of the earth be blessed."

Avraham is also to be found in equal intervals in five other places:

Bereishit 14:5 ואת-הזוזים interval 20

ה וּבְאַרְבַּע עֶשְׂרֵה שָׁנָה בָּא כְדָרְלָעֹמֶר, וְהַמְּלָכִים אֲשֶׁר אִתּוֹ, וַיַּכּוּ אֶת-רְפָאִים בְּעַשְׁתְּרֹת

5 And in the fourteenth year came Chedorlaomer and the kings that were with him, and smote the Rephaim in Ashteroth-

קַרְנַיִם, וְאֶת-הַזּוּזִים בְּהָם; וְאֵת, הָאֵימִים, בְּשָׁוֵה, קִרְיָתָיִם.

karnaim, and the Zuzim in Ham, and the Emim in Shaveh-kiriathaim,

ו וְאֶת-הַחֹרִי, בְּהַרְרָם שֵׂעִיר, עַד אֵיל פָּארָן, אֲשֶׁר עַל-הַמִּדְבָּר.

6 and the Horites in their mount Seir, unto El-paran, which is by the wilderness.

ז וַיָּשֻׁבוּ וַיָּבֹאוּ אֶל-עֵין מִשְׁפָּט, הוא קָדֵשׁ, וַיַּכּוּ, אֶת-כָּל-שְׂדֵה הָעֲמָלֵקִי-- וְגַם, אֶת-הָאֱמֹרִי, הַיֹּשֵׁב, בְּחַצְצֹן תָּמָר.

7 And they turned back, and came to En-mishpat--the same is Kadesh--and smote all the country of the Amalekites, and also the Amorites, that dwelt in Hazazon-tamar.

Bereishit 27:9 אתם **א** interval 43

ט לֶךְ-נָא, אֶל-הַצֹּאן, וְקַח-לִי מִשָּׁם שְׁנֵי גְּדָיֵי עִזִּים, טֹבִים; וְאֶעֱשֶׂה אֹתָם מַטְעַמִּים לְאָבִיךָ, כַּאֲשֶׁר אָהֵב.

9 Go now to the flock, and fetch me from thence two good kids of the goats; and I will make them savoury food for thy father, such as he loveth;

י וְהֵבֵאתָ לְאָבִיךָ, וְאָכָל, בַּעֲבֻר אֲשֶׁר יְבָרֶכְךָ, לִפְנֵי מוֹתוֹ.

10 and thou shalt bring it to thy father, that he may eat, so that he may bless thee before his death.'

יא וַיֹּאמֶר יַעֲקֹב, אֶל-רִבְקָה אִמּוֹ: הֵן עֵשָׂו אָחִי אִישׁ שָׂעִר, וְאָנֹכִי אִישׁ חָלָק.

11 And Jacob said to Rebekah his mother: 'Behold, Esau my brother is a hairy man, and I am a smooth man.

יב אוּלַי יְמֻשֵּׁנִי אָבִי, וְהָיִיתִי בְעֵינָיו כִּמְתַעְתֵּעַ; וְהֵבֵאתִי עָלַי קְלָלָה, וְלֹא בְרָכָה.

12 My father peradventure will feel me, and I shall seem to him as a mocker; and I shall bring a curse upon me, and not a blessing.'

יג וַתֹּאמֶר לוֹ אִמּוֹ, עָלַי קִלְלָתְךָ בְּנִי; אַךְ שְׁמַע בְּקֹלִי, וְלֵךְ קַח-לִי.

13 And his mother said unto him: 'Upon me be thy curse, my son; only hearken to my voice, and go fetch me them.'

Bereishit 31:11 הָאֱ-לֹהִים interval 13

יא וַיֹּאמֶר אֵלַי מַלְאַךְ הָאֱלֹהִים, בַּחֲלוֹם-- יַעֲקֹב; וָאֹמַר, הִנֵּנִי.

11 And the angel of God said unto me in the dream: Jacob; and I said: Here am I.

יב וַיֹּאמֶר, שָׂא-נָא עֵינֶיךָ וּרְאֵה כָּל-הָעַתֻּדִים הָעֹלִים עַל-הַצֹּאן,

12 And he said: Lift up now thine eyes, and see, all the he-goats which leap upon the flock are streaked, speckled, and grizzled; for I

עֲקֻדִּים נְקֻדִּים, וּבְרֻדִּים : כִּי רָאִיתִי, אֵת כָּל-אֲשֶׁר לָבָן עֹשֶׂה לָּךְ.

have seen all that Laban doeth unto thee.

Bereishit 34:19 **אביו** interval 16

יט וְלֹא-אֵחַר הַנַּעַר לַעֲשׂוֹת הַדָּבָר, כִּי חָפֵץ בְּבַת-יַעֲקֹב; וְהוּא נִכְבָּד, מִכֹּל בֵּית **אָ**בִיו.

19 And the young man deferred not to do the thing, because he had delight in Jacob's daughter. And he was honoured above all the house of his father.

כ וַיָּבֹא חֲמוֹר וּשְׁכֶם **בְּ**נוֹ, אֶל-שַׁעַר עִירָם; וַיְדַבְּ**רוּ** אֶל-אַנְשֵׁי עִירָם, לֵאמֹר.

20 And Hamor and Shechem his son came unto the gate of their city, and spoke with the men of their city, saying:

כא הָ**אֲ**נָשִׁים הָאֵלֶּה שְׁלֵמִים הֵ**ם** אִתָּנוּ, וְיֵשְׁבוּ בָאָרֶץ וְיִסְחֲרוּ אֹתָהּ, וְהָאָרֶץ הִנֵּה רַחֲבַת-יָדַיִם, לִפְנֵיהֶם; אֶת-בְּנֹתָם נִקַּח-לָנוּ לְנָשִׁים, וְאֶת-בְּנֹתֵינוּ נִתֵּן לָהֶם.

21 'These men are peaceable with us; therefore let them dwell in the land, and trade therein; for, behold, the land is large enough for them; let us take their daughters to us for wives, and let us give them our daughters.

כז וַיְדַבְּרוּ אֵלָיו, אֵת כָּל-דִּבְרֵי יוֹסֵף אֲשֶׁר דִּבֶּר אֲלֵהֶם, **וַיַּרְא** אֶת-הָעֲגָלוֹת, אֲשֶׁר-שָׁלַח יוֹסֵף לָשֵׂאת אֹתוֹ ; וַתְּחִי, רוּחַ יַעֲקֹ**ב** אֲבִיהֶם.

27 And they told him all the words of Joseph, which he had said unto them; and when he saw the wagons which Joseph had sent to carry him, the spirit of Jacob their father revived.

כח וַיֹּאמֶר, יִשְׂרָאֵל, רַב עוֹד-יוֹסֵף בְּנִי, חָי ; אֵלְכָה **וְאֶרְאֶנּוּ**, בְּטֶרֶם אָמוּת.

28 And Israel said: 'It is enough; Joseph my son is yet alive; I will go and see him before I die.'

Genesis Chapter 46 בְּרֵאשִׁית

א וַיִּסַּע יִשְׂרָאֵל וְכָל-אֲשֶׁר-לוֹ, וַיָּבֹא בְּאֵרָ**ה** שָׁבַע ; וַיִּזְבַּח זְבָחִים, לֵאלֹהֵי אָבִיו יִצְחָק.

1 And Israel took his journey with all that he had, and came to Beer-sheba, and offered sacrifices unto the God of his father Isaac.

ב וַיֹּאמֶר אֱלֹהִי**ם** לְיִשְׂרָאֵל בְּמַרְאֹת הַלַּיְלָה, וַיֹּאמֶר יַעֲקֹב יַעֲקֹב ; וַיֹּאמֶר, הִנֵּנִי.

2 And God spoke unto Israel in the visions of the night, and said: 'Jacob, Jacob.' And he said: 'Here am I.'

There is another encoded Avraham, found right at the beginning of the Torah - בראשית ברא א-להים Bereishit 1:1.

Moving the letters of the 2nd and 3rd words around we discover this - " בראשית (In the beginning), אלי (my God), and אברהם (Avraham)…"

Finally, at the beginning of the second account of the creation of heaven and earth (in Genesis 2:4), we find the word בהבראם - moving these letters around gives the implication that both heaven and earth were created solely on account of the generations that would get to discover God through Avraham - באברהם the supreme exemplar of kindness.

These are just a few astounding examples of discovering coded messages from God within His Torah; a clear indication that the purpose of Creation is to reveal to all the people of the world who their Creator really is, and also by implication who they truly are, through these holy teachings passed down by Abraham and his spiritual heirs – the Children of Israel.

Reaching the promised land of self-awareness, by divesting ourselves of acquired negative traits, through introspection and meditation, we can realize ever more of our potential by experiencing the joy of knowing we are made in God's image. In this way, each one of us can unwrap our spiritual present.

"Better to me is the Torah of Your mouth
than thousands in gold and silver" (Psalms 119:72).

Appendix I

How the Exodus story created America

by Michael Freund

Of all the festivals in the Jewish calendar, it is Passover which contains some of the boldest and most powerful imagery.

The departure of our ancestors from Egypt, their pursuit by Pharaoh and his chariots, and the climactic splitting of the Red Sea, are just some of the themes that we continue to celebrate more than 3,300 years later.

Indeed, it is a testimony to the power of Jewish memory as well as the potency of the Passover saga that even after so many generations, we continue to retell and relive this crucial part of our ancient past.

After all, how many other nations on earth go to such great lengths to reenact the experience of their forebears, discussing it in detail late into the night while also trying to instill the next generation with a sense of historical continuity? Clearly, the deliverance of our forefathers from bondage left a deep imprint on the collective psyche of the Jewish people. Our experience with slavery and the yearning for freedom led many Jews of later generations to place themselves at the forefront of various struggles for human liberty and progress.

Not surprisingly, though, the Exodus tale has also ignited the imagination of others throughout history, encouraging them to stand up to tyrants and seek their own liberation.

Perhaps the most resounding instance is to be found in the annals of America and the men who helped to bring it into being, many of whom looked to the story of the exodus for inspiration.

Take, for example, the Pilgrims, who set sail on the Mayflower in September 1620 from the port of Plymouth in southern England in search of a haven where they could practice their religion free of persecution.

As Bruce Feiler, the author of America's Prophet: How the Story of Moses Shaped America, has noted, the Pilgrims viewed themselves as reliving the exodus saga.

"When they embarked on the Mayflower in 1620," Feiler writes, "they described themselves as the chosen people fleeing their pharaoh, King James. On the Atlantic, their leader, William Bradford, proclaimed their journey to be as vital as 'Moses and the Israelites when they went out of Egypt.' And when they arrived in Cape Cod, they thanked God for letting them pass through their fiery Red Sea."

Subsequently, when Bradford wrote Of Plymouth Plantation, his historical account of the Pilgrims' settling of America, he suggested that there were compelling parallels between the experiences of his own community and that of the ancient Israelites.

A decade later, in 1630, a second wave of Pilgrims made their way across the Atlantic on board the Arbella. While en route to the Massachusetts Bay Colony, John Winthrop delivered a sermon to the passengers entitled "A Model of Christian Charity," in which he too invoked comparisons with the Children of Israel.

"We shall find," he said, "that the God of Israel is among us, when 10 of us shall be able to resist a thousand of our enemies, when He shall make us a praise and glory, that men shall say of succeeding plantations: 'The Lord make it like that of New England.'" As if to underline the point, Winthrop concluded his sermon by quoting from "Moses, that faithful servant of the Lord, in his last farewell to Israel."

By all accounts, the Pilgrims were driven by a deep-seated belief that they had a divinely-appointed mission. The early settlers were known to refer to Plymouth colony as "Little Israel," and many spoke of Bradford, who became its governor, as "Moses."

THE MASSACHUSETTS Bay Colony, which was located north of Plymouth, was equally imbued with a strong sense of biblical consciousness and identification.

As Dr. Gabriel Sivan wrote in his monumental work, The Bible and Civilization, "No Christian community in history identified more with the People of the Book than did the early settlers of the Massachusetts

Bay Colony, who believed their own lives to be a literal reenactment of the biblical drama of the Hebrew nation."

The Pilgrims, argues Sivan, saw themselves as "the Children of Israel; America was their Promised Land; the Atlantic Ocean their Red Sea; the Kings of England were the Egyptian pharaohs; the American Indians the Canaanites..."

Moreover, he suggests, they "saw themselves as instruments of Divine Providence, a people chosen to build their new commonwealth on the Covenant entered into at Mount Sinai."

It was this vision and sense of purpose which eventually served as one of the foundations of what came to be known as American Exceptionalism – the belief that the United States is a unique nation blessed by the Creator with a special role to play in the world.

More than a century and a half after the Pilgrims' arrival, the American colonies went to war against their British colonial masters in a struggle for independence, and the revolutionaries were also very much stirred by the story of the Israelites.

In his pamphlet Common Sense, which was published in January 1776 and had a galvanizing effect on American public opinion, Thomas Paine described King George III as the "sullen tempered pharaoh of England."

On July 4, 1776, just moments after formally adopting the Declaration of Independence, the Continental Congress appointed a committee consisting of three illustrious people – John Adams, Thomas Jefferson and Benjamin Franklin – to create "a seal for the United States of America."

On August 20 of that year, the committee members presented their recommendations to the Congress, with Franklin proposing that the seal depict, "Moses standing on the shore, and extending his hand over the sea, thereby causing the same to overwhelm pharaoh who is sitting in an open chariot."

Jefferson suggested a similar theme for the seal, which would portray "The Children of Israel in the wilderness, led by a cloud by day and a pillar of fire by night."

Though neither of these ideas was accepted, the very fact that they were even considered demonstrates the pervasive influence of the biblical exodus on America's Founding Fathers as well as their strong affinity with the story of the Israelites.

Even after the war was over and America gained its independence, this linkage continued to predominate. On March 4, 1805, in his second inaugural address, President Thomas Jefferson said, "I shall need, too, the favor of that Being in whose hands we are, who led our fathers, as Israel of old, from their native land and planted them in a country flowing with all the necessaries and comforts of life."

Jonathan Sacks on Martin Luther King

At the climax of the most remarkable of all his public addresses, the 'I have a dream' speech delivered before the Lincoln Memorial in Washington in 1963, he quoted at length from Isaiah 40:4-5, the passage Jews read on the 'Sabbath of Consolation': 'I have a dream that one day every valley shall be exalted, every hill and mountain shall be made low, the rough places shall be made plain, and the crooked places shall be made straight and the glory of the Lord shall be revealed and all flesh shall see it together.' He added, 'With this faith we will be able to hew out of the mountain of despair a stone of hope.'

…He reminded his audience [in 1968] of the last day of Moses' life. Moses knew that he would not be able to cross the Jordan, to which he had led the people for forty years. God granted him one last gift: not entry into the land, but a glimpse of it from afar, from a mountain-top.

These were almost the last words Martin Luther King spoke that night [in Memphis, Tennessee]: 'We've got some difficult times ahead. But it doesn't matter with me now, because I have been to the mountain-top …And I've looked over. And I've seen the promised land. I may not get there with you. But I want you to know tonight that we as a people will get to the promised land.' It turned out to be the last day of his life too.

Appendix II

THE PROMISED LAND REGAINED

Excerpts from "Stern: THE MAN and HIS GANG"

by Zev Golan

Abraham Stern, called Yair, was the individual who epitomized the beginning of the Jewish revolt against England. His namesake, Elazar Ben-Yair, was the individual who epitomized the end (Masada) of what is known in history as the "Great Revolt" against Rome, almost two thousand years earlier.

The revolt against Rome was ignited by much the same cause as the modern revolt against England. Rome had occupied the country of the Jews, then called Eretz Israel or, alternately, Judea, and ruled with a heavy hand, crucifying Jews throughout its reign. In the year 66, Rome allowed or instigated offenses to Jewish religious sensibilities, and the Jews rose to defend their religious and political independence. England too, occupied the same country, now called Eretz Israel or, alternately, Palestine, ruled with a heavy hand, and in 1928 proscribed Jewish rights to prayer at the Western Wall; then later, rights to immigrate to the land.

Stern and his fighters, and the ninety thousand members of Jabotinsky's Betar youth movement in Poland... faced persecution and death in the 1930s, but they lived simultaneously on Masada with Elazar Ben-Yair and in Modi'in with the Hasmoneans and Maccabees who began there the revolt against the Greeks that culminated in the holiday of Hanukah.

Israel Eldad, Stern's successor as ideologue of Lehi (the Fighters for the Freedom of Israel), wrote in the notebook commentary he gave Stern:

"Healthy is our stock...and it will shake off the dust by the power of its flowing, boiling blood. And with the crumbling of the walls of European and American civilization, the fortress of modern idolatry, the Hebrew nation's stock will stand firm and strong, untouched by worms of rot. The race's fortune was set in the days when Abraham, Isaac, Jacob and Moses blessed it; the race's destiny was set in the days of Isaiah, Amos and Jeremiah; the race's heroism stems from the days of Shimon and Levi and David and the Hasmoneans and the Zealots; the race's culture stems from the days of the sages in Yavneh and those in Tzippori and Usha, the days of Yochanan Ben Zakkai and Rabbi Akiva and Shimon Bar Yochai and Judah the Prince; the race's song began in the days of the Psalms and the prayers of the Kabbalists and the Hasidim. The bearers of the culture of these generations will march proudly and scornfully over the ruins of ancient cultures. They will march toward their destiny..."

Beyond Persecution

The roots of the Hebrew war of liberation were not, contrary to what many well-intentioned friends of Israel and even many Zionists believe, based in a history of persecution. The Abraham that Eldad and Stern knew is not the 100-year-old Abraham afraid he would be killed by neighboring kings who desired his wife, he is the young Abraham as Destroyer wreaking havoc on ancient idol-worshipping civilizations and marching against the current of the ancient world's greatest river toward his destiny. In this history the sons of Jacob, Shimon and Levi, are vigilante brothers avenging the rape of a young Jewish girl. The Talmud's Rabbi Akiva is seen slipping between cities to coordinate military operations and organizing tens of thousands of freedom fighters in a revolt against imperial Rome. The generation of the freedom fighters were weaned on the love songs of Judah HaLevi, the fervent prayer-poems of Elazar the Kalir, and the spiritual energies of the Kabbalists trying to bring redemption from the Galilean city of Safed in the sixteenth century. Lehi's Judaism is alive and drunk with the knowledge of its own destiny.

Though Abraham is more often portrayed today as a spiritual man than the warrior who fought and defeated four kings (a war he fought because one man, his nephew was being held captive by them), his story is available and occasionally read, given its inclusion in the Bible. Rabbi Akiva is studied more for his Talmudic arguments than his heroism, but the story of his death is also familiar, given that he was murdered at the stake in 135 by the Romans who crushed the free Jewish state he helped found. That which comes next, however, is a black hole in Jewish history. Most Jewish day schools, in the

Diaspora and in Israel, fly through the centuries, setting down only on an occasional poet or persecution: the Temple was destroyed, the Jews resigned themselves to their sad fate for two thousand years and became sheep.

To understand Stern one must follow him to Masada. To understand his successor as operations chief of Lehi, Yitzchak Shamir one must know he said he left Europe and moved to Eretz Israel because he was inspired by the heroes of the Bible and specifically, the personality of King David.

The freedom fighters were inspired by a Jewish History that went beyond persecution. "The main and decisive points," perhaps were not to be found in the history books everyone reads, "perhaps they were deliberately omitted...Thus we do not yet have a history with a national foundation." They felt that "the true Hebrew history...has not yet been written."

An article in the second issue of Lehi's underground paper, *Bamachberet,* tells of some of the heroes and would-be heroes of the Jewish people and concludes,

"In all the diasporas of the Exile, the Hebrew people tried in every generation to restore its independence by means of arms. The attempt to paint the life of the Hebrew people in Exile as one huge effort to explain every letter and jot of the Torah, with the most interesting events being argued between rabbis and Karaites, medieval linguistic disputes and the different opinions of Hasidim and their opponents – is a great falsification...A ridiculous theory..."

WAR AND INDEPENDENCE IN THE MIDDLE EAST, 70-1200

As the fighters saw Jewish history, it went something like this: The Jews were committed to national liberation before the destruction of the Temple and their state in the year 70 and remained so afterward. This commitment was most easily and naturally expressed by those Jews who were forcibly relocated to countries adjacent to their native land when it was "cleansed" of Jews by the victorious Romans, while, according to Yalin-Mor, the rebels who survived the Roman massacre of the Jewish forces "fled not to save themselves, but dispersed to all parts of the Roman Empire to every place a Jewish heart beat and organized the continuation of the war, on foreign soil."

So when Rome invaded Armenia in 114, the leader of the Jewish community in the Middle East (known as the Exilarch), Shlomo Ben-Hunya, resisted the local Parthian government's plans to abandon the region to Rome. Instead, he raised a militia to harass the empire to revolt, and rallied them and also the Parthian forces. The Jews were anxious to throw off the yoke of Rome, so they fought for their freedom in Egypt, Cyprus, and today's Libya. This was in effect a second revolt against Rome, following upon the Great Revolt, which had essentially ended with the fall of Jerusalem in the year 70. It took Emperor Trajan about a year to subdue the fighting Jews of this second revolt. He slaughtered as many as he could, and Jews were entirely banned from Cyprus afterward.

A Roman procurator, Lucius Quietus, erected an idol in the ruins of the Temple in Jerusalem and ignited what became known as the Kitos War. He conquered other areas with large Jewish populations, who naturally resisted with the local populace against him. Though Quietus was successful in battle, the wars took their toll on Rome. When Trajan died, his successor, Hadrian, had Quietus executed and abandoned the disputed faraway areas. Rome's enemy, the Parthians, rewarded the Jews for their military prowess, which helped prevent a permanent Roman takeover of their regions, by recognizing the Jewish Exilarchs as princes.

Hadrian proved no friend of the Jews. As Rome had done before the Great Revolt, it attempted once again to impose a foreign culture and value on Judea. In 131, Hadrian changed the name of Judea's capital to the Roman "Aelia Capitolina." He forbade the practice of circumcision and began to reconsecrate the Jewish temple on Mount Moriah in Jerusalem as a temple honoring a Roman god, Jupiter. Shimon Bar-Kochba led a war of independence (in Lehi's words, he "once again raised the banner of revolt in an underground"), which has come to be known as the Third Jewish-Roman War. For almost three years, Bar-Kochba led an independent Jewish state. The coins his government minted were imprinted with images of the Temple and other Jewish national-religious symbols, as well as the name Shimon and slogans such as "Year one (or two) of the redemption of Israel," or "For the freedom of Jerusalem." The Romans defeated the Jews in 135, executing the revolt's rabbinic leadership, including the leading Talmudic scholar, Rabbi Akiva, and wiping out Bar-Kochba's last stronghold, the city of Betar. Hadrian marked the destruction of the Jewish state by changing the land's name from "Judea" to "Syria Palestina," after an ancient people, the Philistines, who had lived along the coast and fought the Israelites in biblical times but who no longer existed. He hoped to erase the

Jewish tie to the land that had until then been known either as Judea or as Israel, but was henceforth known as Palestina, or Palestine.

In 1932, Abba Ahimeir, a writer and historian who influenced and worked with Stern and the underground fighters, wrote that the three revolts against Rome were "stages" in one event: the great Israeli revolution.... The Israeli revolution was a revolution of grand proportion, the likes of which we find in every great historical nation.

The Jewish yearning for independence did not end there. In 351, a revolt broke out in Tzippori in the Galilee, apparently when the Jews recognized their leader as a sovereign king. The revolt spread to Tiberias and was crushed the following year by the Romans.

In 512, a Persian king denied a teenaged Exilarch in Babylon named Mar Zutra II the right to organize Jewish self-defense. Mar Zutra did so anyway, and did not stop there; he raised an army and declared Jewish independence from Persia. He led an army and maintained Jewish independence for seven years. Thus in 513 the Jews had an independent state and a victorious army, four centuries after their destruction of the Temple and after the Bar-Kochba revolt was crushed. In 520, Mar Zutra, then in his twenties, and his father Mar Hanina were defeated in battle and were crucified in the city of Mehoza (in today's Iraq).

The struggle for freedom did not end with Mar Zutra. In 517 Joseph Du Nuwas, Mar Zutra's cousin and a grandson of the Exilarch Huna (the fifth Exilarch so named), whose daughter had married the king of Himyar, crowned himself ruler of this kingdom in the area of today's Medina in Arabia. The Himyar king Abu Karib had earlier converted to Judaism when he married Huna's daughter; upon the king's death, a pagan usurped the crown. Du Nuwas now dispatched him and retook the crown for himself. The local Christians revolted and seized the town; in what Lehi's paper called "the great war of the Hebrew king Joseph Du Nawas, Du Nuwas defeated them, too. Christians in the northern town of Najrab. took up arms against him. When his peace offer was refused, he laid siege to Najrab and eventually executed all the rebels. He then insisted that all the Christians in his kingdom pay a tribute as financial compensation for the persecution of the Jews in Christian areas.

Du Nawas' natural ally in the war against Rome would have been Persia, but the Persian king had already crucified Mar Zutra and did not care to support an armed Jewish fighting force anywhere. In 525 the Romans joined with their allies the Ethiopians and attacked by sea; Du Nawas laid chains across the landing sites but was unable to prevent the armies' landing. With the Romans and Ethiopians attacking by sea and local Christians attacking on land, he was greatly outnumbered. Rather than surrender, he rode his horse off a cliff into the sea.

Mar Zutra and Du Nawas lived relatively near to their ancestral land, and they were imbued with a commitment to liberty as well as the more well-known Jewish commitment to the God of Israel. They were also imbued with the fighting spirit and skills of their ancestors. This same spirit soon animated another scion of the Exilarch's family, Nehemiah.

In 602 or 603 a Roman rebel named Phocas overthrew and killed the Emperor Maurice, and then fought a war with the Persian king, Khosrau. Khosrrau wished to enlist the Jews as an ally. He gave them civil and religious rights, reopened the great rabbinical academies, and appointed Nehemiah, son of the Exilarch Husha, as Commander in Chief of his Persian armies. Nehemiah raised an army of twenty thousand troops. A Jewish prince was now leading a Jewish-Persian army against Rome, over five hundred years after the destruction of the Jewish state.

Some time later, as the battles continued, Phocas was overthrown and the new emperor decided to counteract the Exilarch's influence by appointing a priest as head of his own army. The Persian-Jewish-Roman war then became a Zoroastrian-Jewish-Christian war.

A wealthy Jewish leader, Benjamin of Tiberias, took the opportunity to raise an army of his own to fight for Jewish independence in the Holy Land. The Jews of Tiberius, Nazareth, and the entire Galilee marched on Jerusalem with a Persian division supporting them. The Jews of southern Eretz Israel joined, as did some Arabs. In 614, the Jewish-Persian army conquered Jerusalem. Nehemiah was made ruler of the Holy City. He began preparing to rebuild the Temple. Some months later, before he could do so, he was killed, along with his ruling council and many other Jews, by Christians. The rest of the Jews fled to Caesaria.

From there they launched another attack on Jerusalem and once again took the city. They also attacked Tyre and other cities. They besieged Tiberias, conquering it 20 days later. In 625, the city was retaken by Byzantium. The Byzantines killed many of the Jewish rebels, but amnestied Benjamin in 628. Nonetheless, for 14 years the Jews had been free from Christian domination. The sad end to this story is that Khosrau betrayed the Jews, allowing the Romans to kill thousands outside Jerusalem. The Jews realigned themselves with Rome, but to no avail; the Romans, too, betrayed them. The ironic outcome was that Nehemiah's brother was sold as a slave; he accepted the leadership of a newcomer to local politics, Mohammed, and became Mohammed's top military man, named Solomon Farsi, in which role he led an army of Jews and Arabs against Byzantium in the part of Palestine that is today the Hashemite Kingdom of Jordan.

In about the year 700, another relative of the Exilarchs, Isaac Ovadia, known to Persians as Abu Issael Isfahani (and nicknamed Abu Issi) defeated the Persians in battle – according to one report, when surrounded he drew a circle around his troops and the enemy amazingly retreated – and announced he would play a messianic role in history. Shortly afterward he himself fell in the war he initiated.

In 720 Jews from as far away as Spain flocked to Syria in response to the call of Serenus the son of Jacob the son of Isaac (this latter being an Exilarch), who was on his way to try to conquer the Jewish homeland. Though fighting for the Land of Israel, he himself did not abide by Jewish law and probably rejected much Jewish doctrine as well. He was defeated by Khalif Yazid II.

David Alroy was born in 1160 in Kurdistan. He also claimed to be a descendent of an Exilarch. He announced that he would free the Jews from foreign control and liberate Jerusalem. He took up arms against the Arab rulers of what is today Iraq, won a major battle in Mosul, was joined by Jewish fighters from Azerbeijan and Baghdad, and won a series of battles before his own death on the battlefield.

Clearly, the Jews expelled from their native land not only longed to restore their country but made real efforts to do so. Sometimes they succeeded and returned to the Jerusalem they loved, other times they died on battlefields from which their city could only be seen with an inner eye. Such attempts to return home were most common in the first millennium of the Common Era, in areas bordering Eretz Israel. As time passed, the Jews were dispersed further afield. In these countries, too they were not the passive persecuted they are often imagined.

Raising Flags and Armies in Europe, 1500-1666

One of the more infamous Christian persecutions of Jews is the Inquisition, during which Jews were forced to convert to Christianity. Some Jews continued to worship the Jewish God in secret (those who did were called Marranos). But not all were reduced to worshipping in rooms with their curtains drawn.

Juan de Abadia, for example, organized a team of six other men that assassinated the chief inquisitor of Saragosa. The torturer always wore armor around his torso and head; the conspirators followed him to church and when he knelt they stabbed him in the neck. Juan killed himself in prison. Most of his comrades were tortured and died at the stake.

Emanuel Da Costa posted a placard on the door of the Cathedral of Lisbon in February 1539. In defiance of the Christian authorities burning Jews and at the risk of his life, Da Costa wrote: "The messiah has not yet appeared," and attacked Christian deceit. The king and the pope offered rewards of thousands of ducats for information leading to his arrest. When arrested, he confessed and was tortured on the rack and burned at the stake.

"Caesar's Rome could not subdue [the Jews'] faith and loyalty and neither could papal Rome's Inquisition. When heroes are presented as educational examples and paragons, the fighter will learn to walk in their paths and not the paths of betrayal," wrote Yalin-Mor in a Lehi newspaper.

Into the cauldron of misery and torture in Europe, a messenger from the Jewish past and future emerged: David Hareubeni (David the Reubenite) had traveled from Arabia, he explained, where he was brother to a Jewish king. He said he had been sent to win European Christian assistance for his hundreds-of-thousands-strong Jewish army so that it could expel the Turks from the Jewish homeland. He rode into Rome on a white horse, was received by Pope Clement VII, and won his support. Hareubeni next journeyed to Portugal to win King John III's support; here, too, he arrived royally with flags flying and a royal retinue. John, desiring to have Hareubeni and the Jews as an ally, promised

Hareubeni eight ships and thousands of guns, and apparently delayed for a time the planned persecution of his own Jews. Hareubeni did not have an easy time of it, though, in such desperate times. He was arrested in Spain, released by the intervention of the Emperor Charles, traveled to areas under papal jurisdiction, and ended up back in Rome. He negotiated with the Venetian senate. In Ratisbon he asked the emperor to allow Marranos to arm themselves and join the Jewish army in order to free the Jewish homeland from the Turks. This was too much for the emperor, and the plans for a army of liberation in 1532 amounted to naught. Hareubeni was put in prison and probably died there. "Hareubeni saw himself in the role of a liberation movement, an irredendist movement, a movement to restore the homeland to its owners," wrote Lehi.

One young youth inspired by Hareubeni was Shlomo Molcho. Molcho dropped his family's pretense of Christianity and returned to the fold. He circumcised himself and fled the Inquisition, finding safety in Turkey. He became a Kabbalist and studied with one of its masters, Joseph Taytasak, and he himself inspired Joseph Karo, author of the *Shulchan Aruch* (Code of Jewish Law), to become an adept of Kabbalah. Molcho journeyed to Rome, lived in rags as a beggar, had several visions, and proclaimed that a great flood would strike the city and an earthquake in Portugal. These indeed came to pass, in 1530 and 1531, respectively. Molcho spoke publicly in synagogues and created his own flag, under which he and thousands of Jews marched, expecting redemption. Early in 1531, when the Inquisition insisted on laying its hands on him, the pope helped him escape from Rome. Hareubeni had been imprisoned for trying to convince the emperor to arm Jews; when Molcho was finally caught he could not claim the diplomatic immunity of Hareubeni. Molcho was condemned to burn at the stake. Afraid he would sway the crowds that had come to watch, the Inquisition led him to his death gagged. But at the last minute, a messenger arrived with a message from the emperor: if Molcho would return to the Church he would be spared. The gag was removed. Molcho replied that he had always desired to die a martyr's death. His flag can still be viewed today, in the Jewish Museum in Prague.

Two Jewish leaders widely remembered today are Donna Gracia Nasi and her nephew and son-in-law, Don Joseph Nasi (Joseph the Prince). She was born in 1510 to a Marrano family. She and her husband ran banking and shipping companies, when he died, she took over. When her brother died, she took over his banking operations, too. She became one of the wealthiest people in

Europe; her bribes to the pope delayed the introduction of the Inquisition into Portugal for some time. She herself had to flee several cities in order to stay alive. In 1553 she moved to Istanbul. There, her daughter married Don Joseph Nasi.

He was born in Spain after the expulsion of its Jews, also to a Marrano family. He fled ahead of the enmity of local rulers or the Inquisition; first to Portugal, then Antwerp, France, Venice, and finally Istanbul. There he was a sort of foreign minister, negotiating peace between the Ottomans and Poland and heavily involved in the wars with Venice and between the Netherlands and Spain. The Ottoman Sultan Selim appointed him Duke of Naxos.

In 1558, just under one thousand years after Benjamin of Tiberias and his Jewish forces lost the city, Donna Gracia leased Tiberias from the Sultan. In 1561, Don Joseph attempted to realize his dream of rebuilding his homeland: the sultan gave him permission to resettle Tiberius. Don Joseph rebuilt the city and its walls and spent a small fortune trying to turn it into a self-supporting town. Eventually another war intervened and plans for a Jewish resettlement there had to be abandoned.

The next major attempt to restore the Jews to their homeland had an even more unfortunate conclusion. Shabtai Zvi proclaimed himself messiah in 1665. The entire Jewish world and much of the Christian followed his every step with great enthusiasm. Jews sold their homes and property in order to prepare for the journey to Eretz Israel. For reasons still unknown, during a conversation with the sultan the next year he converted to Islam. He is known as the mystical messiah, who thought to bring redemption not by means of arms but by use of the Kabbalah. Because of the debacle resulting in his failure, the Lehi's Eldad believed that Shabtai Zvi made a contribution to actualizing Jewish sovereignty: the Jewish people learned that if they wanted to be redeemed, they would need to do more than pray and rely on Heaven. Stern's fellow-poet Uri Zvi Greenberg, another father of the underground, mentions Shabtai Zvi in several of his poems. In World War I, as a soldier, he even troubled himself to visit Shabtai Zvi's grave when it was within range and banged with his rifle butt on the tomb, calling a greeting to the would-be redeemer. Greenberg and many of the fighters saw all those who dreamed and worked for redemption as kindred spirits. In an underground newspaper published in 1943, Lehi wrote, "Shabtai Zvi intended to realize the messianic longings of Israel. Both were born of the deep, vital internal root of the Polish rebellions. Of course, their failure is no yardstick.... (In the 1970's Eldad gave a course entitled "Zionism As a Messianic Movement That Is a Continuation of Previous Messianic Movements.")

Flags and Armies from the Galilee to Jerusalem 1697-1938

Thirty years after Shabtai Zvi and exactly two hundred before Theodor Herzl, Jews from the Diaspora began returning to their land, to the Jewish communities of Hebron, Jerusalem, Safed, Tiberias, and other cities in which Jews had continued to live since biblical times. Rabbi Judah Hasid organized and led a march of fifteen hundred Jews to Eretz Israel in 1697. It took them three years and only one thousand survived the journey. Rabbi Judah Hasid himself died about a week after their arrival in Jerusalem; he was 41 years old. The freedom fighters did not see Theodor Herzl, whose 1896 book *The Jewish State* sparked modern political Zionism, and who created the Zionist movement by staging the First Zionist Congresss in 1897, as a quirk in Jewish history. They saw him as another Hareubeni, another Molcho. They said so explicitly:

"Herzl spoke in the name of the Hebrew people, though in reality the people did not yet exist in terms of a body ready to act, rise, make aliya, conquer, and settle; in actuality there were only individuals.... [Hareubeni's] 'fib' about a messenger from a Hebrew army is no more a "fib" than Herzl saying he represented the Jewish people. And Hareubeni undoubtedly saw the tribes of Hebrew fighters, which still existed in his time, and they gave him the idea. Potentially, a Jewish army could have been established in Europe; in reality things were different; in reality, David Hareubeni had only a handful of 'pioneers,' to use our word."

Like Hareubeni and Molcho, Herzl had the gall to negotiate with a pope and with an emperor (in his case, the Kaiser). The fighters saw themselves as heirs to this tradition. And, since many newcomers to Lehi were encountering for the first time the opposition of their families and the leaders of establishment Zionism. Lehi emphasized that Hareubeni, Molcho, and Herzl had met with opposition from the establishment Jews of their times: "Anyone who carefully reads the story of David Hareubeni and his diaries from Italy, Spain and Portugal, will find in them much to compare with the tragic parts of Herzl's diary. The internal front each faced was much tougher than the external."

Herzl's greatness was in overcoming or circumventing the opposition of assimilationist well-to-do Jews and turning the desire of the Jewish masses into a political movement. He turned the existing settlement movement and the "redemption" of parcels of land into tools harnessed to create a state. Like Molcho before him, he raised a flag and knew the Jewish people would follow him home to Zion. Once, he responded to a taunt that he would fail as Molcho had by noting that Molcho did not have trains.

Herzl was the first in a line of modern heroes emulated by the underground fighters. They admired the scope of his vision and his political genius. Herzl died in 1904, at the age of 44, sure his vision would become reality. The next big step toward this vision was made by a group of Jews in Palestine during World War I, a time when the Ottoman Empire still ruled the country. These include Aharon Aaronsohn, an agronomist who had won worldwide fame when he discovered wild wheat, the prototype for cultivated wheat (he made the discovery in the north of Eretz Israel); Aharon's sister, Sarah, who had seen the Turkish massacre of the Armenian people as she travelled from Constantinople back to the Galilee; Absalom Feinberg, a poet engaged to the Aaronsohn sibling Rivka, and perhaps in love with Sarah; Joseph Lishansky, a champion horse rider and shootist respected by local Arabs as one of their own; and several others based around the Aaronsohn agricultural center in Zichron Yaacov. They combined to form a group they called Nili, which is the Hebrew acronym for "The Eternal One of Israel Will Not Lie" (meaning Heaven will help free the land).

Nili became a spy network operating for the British behind Ottoman lines. They believed the Turks would just as soon kill the Jews as they had the Armenians, and that only a British victory would allow the Jews to attain independence in Eretz Israel. They risked their lives to gather data attained about Axis troop movements, which they sent to British headquarters in Egypt. Members of Nili were arrested and escaped from jail, were hunted by the Turks and by Jews afraid they were endangering the community, crossed the Sinai Desert by camel and foot to ensure the British would get their reports, swam to and from British boats idling miles offshore, and were eventually undone by a carrier pigeon that landed among the Turks with Nili's coded reports. Feinberg had already been killed in a skirmish with Beduin in Sinai. Sarah Aaronsohn committed suicide while being tortured by the Turks. Lishansky and Naaman Belkind were hanged. Aharon was out of the country when the ring was discovered. At war's end he headed to the Peace Conference to press his claims for Jewish statehood. His plane went down over the English Channel for reasons unexplained. According to the man in charge of Near East Intelligence in the British War Office during the war, General Allenby's successful conquest of Palestine was "largely owing" to Nili's work.

Joseph Trumpeldor was another World War I figure who established a fighting unit to assist the British. He – with Jabotinsky, and as Aaronsohn – knew that if the Jews were to have a place at the peace negotiations after the war, they would need to earn it by their deeds in the war, the same as any of the Allies. He – as Jabotinsky and Aaronsohn – knew that an Allied victory was a necessary step in the direction of Jewish statehood. Trumpeldor was born in 1880. He was the only Jewish officer in the Russian army before the Russian revolution. He lost an arm in the Russo-Japanese War, in the Battle of Port Arthur. He moved to Palestine and was among the many Jews deported to Egypt by the Turks during World War I. In Alexandria he met Jabotinsky and the pair agitated for the establishment of a Jewish Legion within the British army, dedicated to the liberation of Palestine. The British offered a corps to fight the Turks elsewhere; Jabotinsky went to London to continue pressing for a Legion, while Trumpeldor accepted the proposal.

Raphael Abulafia, who served in the corps (and, after he was wounded in Nili) recalled that the Jewish troops who enlisted in Egypt "expected to leave for Gaza to take Eretz Israel from the Turks." As their boats readied to sail, they and their families and the others who had come to see them off sang the *Hatikva*. "But later we didn't see Gaza, only water and sky. So we expected to land at Tel Aviv. But we only saw water and sky. We hoped we were heading for Haifa. But – only water and sky. Finally we saw the Greek Isles and on April 25 landed with British forces from many other countries in Gallipoli.

Trumpeldor led the seven hundred Jews who had volunteered. They fought at Gallipoli in 1915 as a transport unit known as the Zion Mule Corps. After the British defeat in Gallipoli, the unit was disbanded.

The British still refused to create the Legion Jabotinsky was lobbying for, so, following the Russian Revolution, Trumpeldor headed to Russia to see if he could talk the Russians into establishing a Legion. He knew the new liberal and socialist Russian government viewed favourably and hoped to recruit volunteers to fight Turkey. After receiving encouragement from Deputy

Minister of War Boris Savinkov, he submitted a detailed plan to the government to raise an army of one hundred thousand Jews. Before anything could be done, the Bolsheviks overthrew the government.

At the same time, England had invaded Palestine and issued the Balfour Declaration supporting the right of the Jewish people to the country. Trumpeldor decided he no longer needed an army. Since, in any case, he could no longer expect the support of the Russian government, he instead promoted an "army" of one hundred thousand pioneers who would march from Russia to Eretz Israel to build the country. He spent a year and a half organizing tens of thousands of these pioneers, then returned to his home in Eretz Israel to get the country ready for their arrival.

By the time the chaos of the revolution had subsided and they could travel, the Russian government had decided they should not be allowed to do so and sealed the borders. Until then Trumpeldor had imagined massive marches and sailing; now only a trickle of pioneers managed to escape. Meanwhile, Eretz Israel had devolved into chaos. The border areas were contested by the British and French, and local Arabs were pillaging and battling. Trumpeldor took command of a fort in the Galilee called Tel Hai and met his death there, shot in the stomach by Arabs. His dying words, recorded by his doctor, were, "It does not matter, it is good to die for one's country."

Trumpeldor's stoic death inspired the youth and he became a national hero. Trumpeldor's name was incorporated by Jabotinsky in the name of his youth movement, which he called Brit Trumpeldor (usually called by its acronym, Betar). The Lehi underground, which was created two decades after Trumpeldor's death, and which included many members of Betar, both admired and differentiated itself from Trumpeldor. The Lehi fighters believed that goals and methods needed to change with the times, and Trumpeldor's image was too "defensive" for the underground. Nonetheless, they compared him to Stern: Both wanted to raise an army of tens of thousands in the Diaspora and bring it to Eretz Israel; Trumpeldor acted alone, with only Jabotinsky at his side, to establish the fighting legions, as Stern acted against the wishes of the establishment Zionists in order to create the underground; both Trumpeldor and Stern had the courage to stand alone, under-armed and outnumbered by the enemy; and both faced their end alone, at the head of a small group with no home front behind them.

In London, after Trumpeldor had left the Zion Mule Corps, Jabotinsky succeeded in organizing the Jewish Legion. He enlisted in it as a soldier and fought in the battle to liberate Palestine. Jabotinsky had hoped the Legion would become the nucleus of a Jewish army that would remain there after the war, but the British balked at the idea. After Trumpeldor's death in 1920, Jabotinsky recruited some Legion veterans and many Jerusalem youth and created a self-defense unit called the Hagana. He planned to protect Jerusalem's Jews from an attack similar to the one in the Galilee that killed his friend. This the Hagana did – six Jews were murdered in the Old City where the British forbade the Hagana to operate, but Jabotinsky's Jewish forces protected newer Jewish neighbourhoods. Jabotinsky was arrested for this, charged with possession of weapons and inciting segments of the population against each other, and sentenced to 15 years hard labor. On appeal the verdict was quashed and he and his 19 co-defendants were exonerated. By 1929 Jabotinsky had been barred by the British from entering Eretz Israel and the Hagana had atrophied. When Arabs attacked Jews, scores were killed throughout the country. The activist elements of the Hagana left and created the Irgun, making Jabotinsky their "supreme commander."

When Arabs began murdering Jews again in the mid-1930s, the Irgun commanders, Jabotinsky included, did not know how to respond. Some advocated reprisal attacks; others opposed this in principle and in practice. So. Jabotinsky, too, was both admired and yet left behind by the Sternists. In 1938, Irgunist Shlomo Ben-Yosef was hanged by the British for a reprisal attack on Arabs near Rosh Pina, and his name entered the pantheon of Jewish martyrs stretching back to Molcho and Rabbi Akiva.

Jabotinsky had chosen as a slogan for the Betar movement the name of Trumpeldor's fort, and Betar members greeted and parted from each other not with *shalom* (hello) but with "Tel Hai." After the British hanged Ben-Yosef in the Acco Fortress Prison and a would-be Jewish immigrant drowned near Gaza trying to get past British patrols, Uri Zvi Greenberg suggested adopting a new slogan, "Gaza-Acco," symbolizing a move from the defensive position implied by "Tel Hai" to a readiness to do whatever is necessary to free the homeland.

This was the history that Stern new and taught. One attempt after another through the centuries, the millennia, to liberate the homeland from foreign rule, whoever the foreigner: Roman, Persian, Byzantines, Christians, Moslems, Turks, British. Bar-Kochba passed the baton to myriads of dreamers, and the members of Lehi saw themselves as part of a chain, the only legitimate link left. In a 1943 memorial article, Lehi wrote, "Ben-Yosef! The Fighters for the Freedom of Israel do not hold ceremonies at your grave. This is not the time for the people of Israel to hold ceremonies. The Fighters for the Freedom of Israel are faithful to your path. Only we few."

How is This Zionism Different from All Other Zionisms?

On the one hand the Lehi fighters' belief that they were the few proponents of Jewish goals in Zion – and their self-image as a select few – may seem absurd, given the existence of, in their own time, almost fifty years of Zionist congresses, the Jewish Agency for Palestine, the World Zionist Organization, the National Council of the Jews of Eretz Israel, Zionist youth movements stretching from Jabotinsky's Betar to the socialist Hashomer Hatzair, and hundreds of thousands, if not millions, of Jews who either lived in Eretz Israel or sought to move to there.

On the other hand, the fact cannot be denied that they were few. Only about one thousand of the hundreds of thousands of Jews in Eretz Israel joined Stern or Lehi, and another five thousand joined the Irgun, which during Stern's stint at the helm in the 1930s, and again in the late 1940s, propounded the same kind of Zionism as Lehi.

At the time there were (and today there still are) several forms or schools of Zionism. Practical Zionism, which emphasized creating facts on the ground; Political Zionism, which belittled the value of such facts (farms and homesteads) and sought political recognition and broad political solutions, socialist-Zionism, which sought to create an egalitarian sovereignty run by a socialist party; and Revisionist Zionism, which hoped to revise the minimal Zionist goals of the 1920s and 1930s and return to Zionism's original goals, which it deemed a Jewish state on both sides of the Jordan River, to which endangered Jews from Europe and elsewhere would be evacuated en masse.

Most Zionists were in one way or another either Practical or Political. The Irgun usually derided the former, Lehi derided both and preached revolution. Six thousand fighters out of six hundred thousand – one percent of the Jews in Zion – were Revolutionary Zionists.

Practical Zionism emerged from the Hibat Zion (Love of Zion) movement of the late nineteenth century, which sought to afford Jews from Eretz Israel and from the Exile an opportunity to till and settle the land. The Lovers of Zion, as they were called, purchased land in faraway areas of the country, trained settlers to farm, and its members relocated to these new farmlands. Many died of hunger or malaria and no one, Lehi included, questioned their sacrifices and devotion.

Some of the immigrant settlers emerged from the European Enlightenment and from a semi-socialist desire to make Jews "productive" members of society (i.e. farmers) as opposed to middleclass tradesmen. Because these goals could not be achieved in the lands of Exile, such enlightened socialists sought to return to Zion. This last fact allowed them to join Herzl's political movement, though in most respects they were far from his Political Zionism.

Before Herzl, as Lehi saw things, the Love of Zion had not been focused on a Jewish state. For its members and followers, settlement had become an end in itself. In the years that followed, as they were building towns and farms, they needed a legal framework in which to operate; they also needed to defend their settlements. They saw themselves as a vanguard reclaiming the land but statehood, an army, and other Zionist goals were an afterthought. Herzl refocused the movement on a political goal to be achieved by political means: a state to be won by grand diplomacy.

Political diplomacy, too, emerged from European culture, with its roots in the Emancipation of the Jews from the ghettos. The Emancipation had failed, the Jews remained either discriminated against or in danger. Famously Herzl became a "Zionist" when he witnessed crowds of "enlightened" French citizens calling for death to all Jews when a French Jewish soldier, Alfred Dreyfus, was falsely accused of treason. Political Zionists did not demand that one particular nation recognize the rights of its Jews but that, internationally, the rights of the Jewish nation be recognized. This essentially meant that the right of the Jewish people to a homeland be recognized. While the tools of the Political Zionists were legal and diplomatic, and they included Zionist congresses, rallies, and petitions to foreign governments.

Implied by the tools adopted by Political Zionism was faith in the world's conscience. The Lehi fighters were critical of the hopes pinned by Political Zionists on international conferences held to consider the plight of the Jews and find solutions for Jewish refugees. At a Betar conference in Warsaw in 1938, Menachem Begin spoke about taking up arms to liberate the homeland and was chastised by Jabotinsky, who compared him to a squeaky door serving no purpose. Future Lehi leader Eldad spoke shortly afterward and reminded Jabotinsky that sometimes a squeaky door alerts one to the presence of thieves. Jabotinsky told Begin that if he did not believe in the world's conscience he had no option but to drown himself in a local river. Begin and Eldad did not have any faith in the world's conscience; the British appeasement of Germany, the world's acquiescence to the dismemberment of Czechoslovakia, and the shipping of Jewish refugees back into the Holocaust would soon prove them right, but they had no wish to drown themselves. Instead they chose Revolutionary Zionism.

Revolutionary Zionism differs from Practical and Political Zionism in its ends as well as its means. Both Practical and Political Zionism had within them different ideas about their end goals. In addition to farmers and socialists, Practical Zionism also included "Cultural Zionists." They were led by Asher Ginzberg (known by his pen name, Ahad Ha-am), who thought it obvious that even were a Jewish state to be established, Eretz Israel could never absorb a million refugees in a short period. Thus, he reasoned, pursuing mass emigration from the Diaspora was pointless just as was pursuing a Jewish state. He felt that an elite should move to Eretz Israel, there to develop the cultural aspects of Judaism, so that when a Jewish state would be formed in the distant future, it would have a truly "Jewish" character.

Within Political Zionism, some based their commitment to a Jewish state on the catastrophe awaiting the Jews of the Diaspora. Antisemitism was the major factor in the thinking of these Zionists. Max Nordau was Herzl's deputy in the days of the First Zionist Congress. In 1920 he called for evacuating half a million Jews to Eretz Israel; he was ignored by the Practical Zionists who had taken over the movement after Herzl's death. Nordau was not the only one concerned about a catastrophe on the immediate horizon; for many Zionists, Zionism existed solely to provide a "safe haven" for persecuted Jews. The French public's behaviour toward Dreyfus proved to Herzl that even in a civilized country such as France, antisemitism can still sway the masses. Jabotinsky played on this theme when he wrote of different kinds of antisemitism ("of people" and "of things"), one of which would destroy Polish Jewry. Throughout the 1920s and 1930s the *New York Times* was full of reports of pogroms, economic persecution and hardship, hunger, and other plights affecting millions of Jews. In Russia and the East, the Jews had suffered from pogroms and social discrimination for generations. Some Jews responded by fighting for their rights in these countries. Other Jews believed that if socialism would triumph, the workers' governments would no longer persecute Jews. Zionists believed the solution to the Jewish problem was to leave the countries in which Jews were a minority and establish a Jewish state.

Revolutionary Zionism rejected all these goals. Its proponents did not want to be on the international agenda as a refugee problem; they wanted to be a player in the international arena. To ask others for recognition meant to consider the Jews as objects, not subjects. The Revolutionary Zionists did not focus on the Jews as objects of anything, including persecution. Lehi had not come, the fighters wrote, for individual Jews, but for the Jewish people as a unit, a political subject. They cared not whether a Jew escaped from one country in the Diaspora to another, to them that would be a temporary haven, because the fate of the Jews in any Diaspora is sealed in advance. In the 1940's Lehi claimed to speak not for victims of European or German persecution but in the name of all the victims of all the Exiles as well as those Jews who would be persecuted in Eretz Israel, too, in the future, if they did not succeed in establishing the Hebrew kingdom they sought.

They did not see the Jewish people as an object with problems, but a subject with desires. They described what they wanted as redemption.

In one newspaper article, they wrote that Zionists until then regarded "redeeming the land" as an economic project with a philanthropic aim (to provide land for Jews in trouble). But they said, no other nation purchased its own land in order to solve a social problem. They asked, "What are the Poles, the French, and the Greeks fighting for? To solve a Polish, French, or Greek problem?...Can one imagine a French person convincing someone that he is fighting for a free France because he has no other place to live?" For the Sternists, the homeland was not a solution to the Jewish problem. It was not a safe haven or an "orphanage," not even a place to be settled or defended, it was the object of national desire, and its purpose was to be liberated. After that, an ingathering of the Exiles would be possible and then it would be settled.

The Lehi leaders explained that a belief that Zionist goals would be achieved by settling the land acre by acre and seeking international recognition was a "foolish superstition." A belief that petitions or protests would bring results or that antisemites would be moved by cogent arguments was a "fantasy." They rejected these tenets of establishment Zionism, as unrealistic, just as they rejected the socialist-Zionists' claim that making Jews "productive" would lead to redemption; instead, they argued, redemption would lead to the Jews becoming as productive as necessary. They mocked the claim of the Practical Zionists that each new settlement or factory was a step toward sovereignty; new settlements and factories found favour in Lehi's eyes only because they could be used as springboards for liberating more territory. Nonetheless, Lehi warned that this benefit came at a great cost: it blinded Jews to the fact that their enemies were growing stronger while they were engaged in building an individual settlement or factory. Political Zionists thought they could turn to the world to prevent the enemy from attacking, Lehi believed that the world had no conscience, and the duty of Zionism was not to pressure others to act on one own's behalf; and Jewish arms were not for defending Jews, but for crushing an enemy.

For Lehi, sovereignty was not a solution but a goal, an expression of Jewish culture, as any nation-state is the expression of a people's culture. The few hundred Lehi fighters of 1943 declared themselves determined to fight a war to liberate the homeland from the foreigner; it mattered not to them whether this foreigner was Turk, as it had been, British as it was then, or someone else in the future. They wished to "establish the Jewish kingdom based on our historic rights, on our national desire as expressed in all messianic longings and attempts."We have within us Shlomo Molcho, Joseph Nasi, and Mordecai M. Noah, but our stock is that of David Hareubeni," they wrote.

This obviously incomplete gene pool includes one man who united the Jews under his flag (Molcho), two diplomats (Nasi and Noah, an American consul and journalist who tried to establish a Jewish state on Grand Island in New York in 1825), and primarily Hareubeni, who operated during an age of persecution but who hailed from lands not feeling the whip, and whose goal was not to save unfortunate Jews but to exploit international politics to liberate the homeland by force. The Sternists were not Zionists because they were fleeing something, they were running toward their goal; they were not moved by fear but love.

For them, then, Zionism was not to be justified by the Holocaust. That they, and the Irgun and Hagana, fought to create a Jewish state in the 1940's during and after the Holocaust is a coincidence made lamentable by two facts: First, one of their goals, the creation of a Jewish state, was realized too late to save the Jews of Europe; secondly, the Jews of Europe were trapped and unable to participate in the war of liberation, then murdered and unable to assist the Jewish state in the making. Had they been able to participate, the Jews of Eretz Israel would have much greater numerical and qualitative advantage over their enemies. The small size of the state in 1948 directly reflects the missing millions of brothers and sisters, hundreds of thousands of whom would have come to Eretz Israel, many of these wanted to join the underground, many others would have served in the army, built factories and towns, and contributed their material and spiritual talents to the efforts to create and later preserve the state.

That the war to liberate the homeland had nothing to do with the Holocaust was stated by Lehi; the evidence for this claim is found in the dates. "Practical Zionism" (it was not yet called "Zionism") began as mass emigration long before German antisemitism became dangerous. Rabbbi Judah Hasid sought to hasten redemption by bringing more than a thousand Jews to Eretz Israel in 1700. Three hundred students and followers of the Baal Shem Tov, the founder of modern Hasidism, moved to Safed in 1777, some of them later moving to Tiberias. Five hundred students of Rabbi Elijah of Vilna (known as "the Vilna Gaon") made aliya in 1809; they moved first to Tiberius, then to Safed. By the time this wave of immigration had ended, over five thousand Jews from Eastern Europe and North Africa had come. Throughout the nineteenth and early twentieth centuries, Jews continued to return to the homeland.

"Political Zionism" also began long before the Holocaust (though it, too, had yet to be called "Zionism"). The Sternists generally look to Nili as their first modern predecessor. Nili sprang from the mountains and shores of Eretz Israel and its political and military actions were based on local geopolitical considerations. Nili's Sarah Aaronsohn had been born in the country, in Zichron Yaacov; and Feinberg and Belkind also, in Gedera. Aharon Aaronsohn and Joseph Lishansky had been brought to the country as six year olds. Their goal was not to save refugees, but to liberate the homeland during World War I or immediately thereafter. At the same time, Trumpeldor tried to form an army of one hundred thousand Jews to take the country. The soldiers of the Jewish Legion crossed the Jordan River in British uniform with the same intent, and intended to remain here, as a Jewish army afterward. The Hagana was formed in 1920; the Irgun, in 1931. The justification for Zionism was the desire of the Jewish people to be free in its native land, not the Holocaust.

Stern noted that in the past, the Jews' wars and their struggles for freedom had centered on their religion. The Hasmoneans, Zealots, and Bar-Kochba all fought when foreigners desecrated the nation's sacred grounds. In Exile, the Jewish religion kept the nation alive and provided "citizenship" and a "constitution." The Jewish religion thus provided the ground for Zionism and the Hebrew liberation movement. The blood of the Maccabees flows in the veins of the modern fighters. Even non-observant Jews should therefore respect the Jewish religion.

As for the Temple, it symbolized the nation's spirit. When the Temple fell, the state fell. The state was reconstituted after the Hasmoneans cleansed the Temple. Later the Second Temple fell, and destroyed with it were the Jewish state and homeland. "In the war of the Zealots," wrote Stern, "the Temple became a fortress and it remained the fortress of zealots throughout the ages." The entire nation prayed and continues to pray for its renewal. Thus they will indeed see in its renewal a symbol of the complete redemption.

For most of their lives, the majority of the fighters who served under or with Shamir, Eldad and Yalin-Mor remained what Abraham Stern called anonymous soldiers. Stern had once jotted a note to himself that, "The anonymous have their recompense in the knowledge that they have fulfilled their obligation toward their people and their people's destiny. Their wages have been paid, ahead of them lie – deeds." Shamir had passed a normal man's retirement age before he won a cabinet post. When he became prime minister he was nearly seventy.

But Shamir had to wait that long for recognition partly because for the first three decades of Israel's independence not only the names of Stern's fighters were forgotten but also their deeds, and this, perhaps, would have surprised or offended them more than the fact that their names were missing from the history books. This was no accident, however.

In 1952, Prime Minister Ben-Gurion ordered his government to award military merit badges to everyone he thought worthy, and he listed them all: "All those who did guard duty before Hashomer was founded, the members of Hashomer, the soldiers in the Jewish Legion of World War I, members of the Hagana from the time it was founded until the founding of the IDF [the Israeli army], those who served in the Jewish units of World War II, members of the settlements who were not soldiers in the Israel Defense Forces but who defended the settlements during the War of Independence (Jerusalem, Negba and the like), and all who gave their lives for the homeland though they are not listed above." The Irgun and Lehi (as well as Nili) are conspicuously absent from this purportedly comprehensive list. Ben-Gurion earlier explained his refusal to accord military recognition to dead underground fighters by pointing out he could never equate them with the Hagana. He denied Begin's claim to have had a role in establishing the state, declaring, "This land has a long history. Many foreign regimes were forced from it and yet a Jewish state was not established." He attributed the establishment of the state in 1948 not to the British leaving but to the pioneers who had arrived in the preceding decades and their agricultural work, and he called the Jews' return to physical labor in the fields and construction industry, "perhaps the decisive event that led to the establishment of a Jewish state."

Leftwing politician and Jounalist Uri Avnery mocked the establishment's policy toward the Lehi vets as early as 1958, when he wrote that Ben Gurion and his government think that the removal of the British flag from the country amounts to nothing, but it is thanks to the fighters who brought that flag down that they sit in their government offices.

The British were clear about who drove them from the country. To mark May 14, 1948, the day they terminated their Mandate over Palestine and left the country, they issued the following statement:

"...84,000 troops, who received no cooperation from the Jewish community, had proved insufficient to maintain law and order in the face of a campaign of terrorism waged by highly organized Jewish forces equipped with all the weapons of the modern infantryman. Since the war, 338 British subjects had been killed in Palestine, while the military forces there had cost the British taxpayer 100 million pounds. The renewal of Arab violence on the announcement of the United Nations decision to partition Palestine and the declared intentions of Jewish extremists showed that the loss of further British lives was inevitable. It was equally clear that, in view of His Majesty's Government's decision not to enforce the partition of Palestine against the declared wishes of the majority of its inhabitants, the continued presence there of British troops and officials could no longer be justified.

In these circumstances His Majesty's Government decided to bring to an end their Mandate and to prepare for the earliest possible withdrawal of all British forces."

The statement referred to getting no cooperation from the Jewish community. However, the Hagana and establishment Jewish Agency had cooperated, even turning members of the underground over to the British police. The British referred to a campaign of terror, but the Hagana and Agency had condemned this campaign and often sought to thwart it. From October 1945 until August 1946 they cooperated with the Irgun and Lehi; but before that their members served in the British army and after August 1946 they engaged in only a handful of "terrorist" actions, declaring that they would limit their activities to illegal immigration. The British warned in their statement of the intentions of Jewish extremists who rejected the partition of the country, obviously referring to the Irgun and Lehi, who rejected partition, not to the Hagana and Labor's leadership who accepted it.

The dustbin of history got a shaking with Begin's election to the premiership in 1977, and along with recognition of the accomplishments of Begin's Irgun came recognition of those of Lehi. Arguably, Israelis today may take more pleasure in remembering the Irgunists and the Lehi fighters than in remembering the Hagana, perhaps because revolutions are more exciting than troop movements, prison breaks often excite the imagination more than establishment protests and the total commitment of revolutionaries to a cause seen in stark black-and-white terms stir people.

The Israeli daily *Haaretz* reported in July 2010 that recent years have seen an increased interest in the Irgun and Lehi among the younger generation of Israelis living in Judea and Samaria. *Haaretz* theorizes this generation is attracted by the personalities who sacrificed themselves for Israel. According to the newspaper, at the home of one grandson of an Irgunist, underground songs are sung at Friday evening Sabbath dinners (apparently in addition to the more traditional Sabbath hymns). "I see a connection between the underground members and our generation," the grandson is quoted as explaining. "Both gave their lives for the Land of Israel and the Bible. Yair Stern's beliefs have a lot in common with our own." Another teen living on a settlement said, "The underground movements were a very small group of people who opposed everything accepted in that period. They're like us in a way...We're trying to do something that will make a difference and advance redemption."

"Let Mount Zion rejoice! Let the towns of Judah exult, because of Your judgments. Walk around Zion, circle it, count its towers, take note of its ramparts; go through its citadels, that you may recount it to a future age. For God – He is our God forever. He will lead us for evermore."

Psalms 48:12-15